Trained domestic violence victims' advocate Tracy S. Deitz presents a straightforward guide to ending an abusive or destructive relationship and rebuilding one's life.

–Margaret Lane, Midwest Book Review

"Break The Cycle" provides a wealth of knowledge and is a toolbox full of resources for battered women in an abusive relationship, and for women who have had the strength and courage to leave an abusive relationship.

–Sylvia H. for Readers Favorite

BREAK the CYCLE

HEALING FROM AN ABUSIVE RELATIONSHIP

BY

Tracy S. Deitz

DEDICATION

For our children,
that they may understand
how the disease of alcoholism affects families
and break the cycle of abuse for future generations.

Contents

Stage Two: Swimming
You begin to establish a separate identity and withdraw from codependent behaviors.

Stage Three: Safe on Shore
You stand firm in your unique identity, staying involved in healthy fellowship with God and other people.

If you are in danger,
what are you willing to do to save yourself?

INTRODUCTION

*Y*ou can't take the craziness anymore. Fear stalks you everywhere you go. You wait nervously, with your heart dancing on razor blades—dreading the next explosion from the person you love. You tiptoe around, hoping to avoid problems, yet you never quite succeed.

And after the inevitable storm settles, you let sugar-sweet apologies lull you into thinking everything will be OK. You accept hollow promises, turning a blind eye to reality. Meanwhile, your heart longs for escape from pain and betrayal. Each new crisis destroys a little more of you, and you wonder why your loved one keeps wounding you.

Didn't you promise yourself the last time, "Never again"? Yet here you are—stuck. Trapped in a quicksand of loyalty, you despair of ever finding a safe place where you are respected and loved.

For years, you've tried to save this person who's drowning in addiction or illness, but all he or she does is pull you under with them. You try to rescue, only to be shocked when he or she clutches onto you in a frenzied grab for survival. Sometimes, to protect yourself, you have to back off, swim for the surface, and catch your own breath.

This book is not about rescuing someone else; it's about saving yourself. It's about gathering enough courage and faith to swim into deep water. Stretch toward the horizon you've always longed for but didn't think you could reach. Let the current of God's love carry you to a peaceful shore, where you will discover unexpected strength and value in yourself.

In this book, you will learn how Lydia finally faced the truth about her relationship with an abusive, alcoholic spouse—and how you can find solutions for your situation too. No matter whether your abuser is addicted to substances, has a personality disorder, or is just plain controlling and self-centered, this text shares how to recognize patterns of manipulation and respond in healthier ways.

God used marital separation to lead Lydia to wholeness, restoring her dreams for happiness. And you'll read about a variety of paths God may reveal to you for a more satisfying life. God gave Lydia the ability to change, and he will also help you.

Lydia tells her story in three stages: "Drowning," "Swimming," and "Safe on Shore." The section called "Drowning" addresses how domestic violence begins and reveals common characteristics of a person who has lost individual identity. "Swimming" shows the gradual reawakening of self and withdrawal from abusive situations as you become stronger. "Safe on Shore" covers behaviors that reflect complete confidence to stand on your own. Each chapter ends with a healing practice, questions for private study or small groups, and resources.

Protected with knowledge—and the compassion of others—you too can find victory against abuse. What you choose to do today will affect many future generations.

STAGE ONE:

DROWNING

While trying to cope with the addictive
behavior of another person, you lose your own identity.

CHAPTER ONE

Disconnected

*Y*ou're seeking answers for how to find relief from chaos. You know that things aren't right in your relationship, but you can't figure out what to do. You don't like the damaging situation you're in, but you aren't sure you have what it takes to make changes. Start with one small step at a time by telling someone you trust.

If you are in physical danger or the threat of it, you need immediate, professional assistance. Please call the National Domestic Abuse Hotline at 1-800-799-7233. Be sure to use a phone that cannot be traced to you, in case your call history might be monitored.

You are not alone in facing domestic violence, whether the hazard is physical or emotional. More than seventy thousand victims received help in a single reporting day from 1,746 centers throughout the country.[1] This survey did not count many more people who were too frightened to ask for assistance or were uninformed about resources available.

How do you recognize patterns of abuse? And what can you do to break the cycle of violence?

The emotional stage of drowning occurs when you find your-self reacting to one crisis after another caused by your partner. You feel helpless and experience being victimized in many ways. Traumas with your spouse or partner engulf you to the point that you lose track of who you are.

What most people, including victims, don't realize is the intentional, steady process in which abusers exert— and main-tain— control in an increasingly domineering process. Abusers rarely begin a relationship with violence; instead, they woo with a lightning-swift Hollywood campaign of courtship that knocks the other person off balance and cements an intense emotional attachment.

Abusers often choose partners with generous and gentle natures; then these very attributes become the vulnerable points of attack in an abuser's concerted efforts to establish complete control. A fist isn't necessary to use for domination if put-downs and guilt trips contain a victim. Abusers whittle away at their part-ner's self-esteem until little remains for a victim's self-defense. By the time most people realize that they are in an abusive relation-ship, submission has become an entrenched behavior, and the victim doesn't even know how it all really happened.

Domestic violence is "an epidemic affecting individuals in every community, regardless of age, economic status, race, reli-gion, nationality or educational background," according to the National Coalition Against Domestic Violence.[2] Victims can be male or female.

Gender stereotypes and stigmas often lock families into domestic violence and keep members away from knowl-edgeable sources of help. If you are hesitant to make inquiries because your problem is sensitive, please be reassured that many agencies exist to educate and assist. There is no need to be embarrassed.

The first obstacle to healing is the secrecy surrounding con-cerns. Family members failed to report almost half of the instances of intimate partner violence (IPV) to the police, according to the Bureau of Justice Statistics as reported by researchers.[3]

With silence, the pain will only increase. Hiding problems fre-quently results in more injuries, both emotional and physical. While you hope for better times and try to protect your partner by forgiving unacceptable behavior, in reality, you might be enabling greater destruction of your entire family.

Cycles of abuse are complicated with addictions. Workers serving victims of domestic violence estimate that more than 70 percent of violent incidents in families involve alcohol consumption.[4] If your partner is a heavy drinker, you are at a greater risk of experiencing domestic violence.[5]

"Alcohol is not responsible for the violence—control and power issues are the sources—but alcohol consumption definitely contributes to the problems," said an assistant director of a regional council against domestic violence that serves five counties. She added, "I've been involved with this council for several years. You'd think the instances of domestic violence would have decreased over time. But they haven't. If anything, they're on the rise. Domestic violence is pervasive and a major concern in this country."

Without help addressing abuse and addictions in your family, you can waste years wrestling with insecurity and fear, which is what I did. Not trusting my own judgment, I wondered what to do. As the problems revolving around my husband's drinking escalated, I exhausted myself trying to hold the marriage together. Are you tired too?

Popularity and Addictability of Drugs Among U.S. Adults

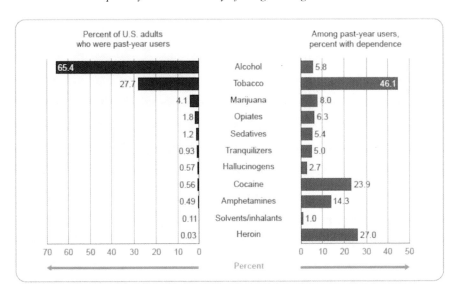

The National Institute of Alcohol Abuse and Alcoholism (NIAAA) estimates eight million people may be dependent users of alcohol. That is nearly five times the number of people dependent on all illicit drugs combined. Chart and statistical analysis reprinted with permission from NIAAA Spectrum, Volume 3, Issue 1, February 2011 as sourced by Grant BF, Dawson DA, Moss HB. Disaggregating the Burden of Substance Dependence in the United States.

Domestic abuse and addiction often occur in tandem, like two wheels on a bicycle flying toward destruction. Ongoing studies have yet to determine if one problem causes the other or vice versa, but that academic discussion doesn't matter much when you find yourself in the middle of a dangerous situation.

Do you find yourself saying things like "if only my spouse wouldn't drink (or use drugs, or watch pornography) anymore, then everything would be all right"?

Denial locks everyone in a place of stagnation that doesn't get better with time. The disease of alcoholism, like any other addiction, is a type of cancer that wraps its tentacles around everyone in the family, creating a toxic environment affecting all members. As the addiction progresses, attention is often focused on the drinker. But family members also become enmeshed battling the twin bullies of shame and secrecy as they cover for the one they love.

The National Institute on Alcohol Abuse and Alcoholism estimates that eight million people may be dependent users of alcohol per year.[6] This number exceeds—by almost five times—the sum of people addicted to all illicit drugs.[7]

Estimates in 2011 from Alcoholics Anonymous show that more than one million people in the United States participate in programs that offer help with alcohol-related problems, and that number includes only those who are willing to work on recovery.[8]

These astounding statistics may be conservative. A projection based on the 2007 National Survey on Drug Use and Health indicated that more than fifteen million people aged twelve and older were dependent on or abused alcohol. Add to this those who used illicit drugs and alcohol, and the sum soared above eighteen million people.[9]

Although not all violent incidents involve addictions, a high correlation exists.[10] Therapists who studied IPV found that half of the couples who sought treatment for substance abuse also reported partner violence in the year before beginning a treatment program.[11]

While substance abuse contributes to family breakdowns, domestic violence is not limited to a single factor. Mental illness, personality disorders (such as narcissism), and cultural expectations about gender roles all can cause abusive situations.

Medical professionals calculate that domestic violence may happen in 25 percent of U.S. families.[12] With the prevalence of IPV, some major medical organizations suggest that physicians make screening for IPV as common as asking patients if they smoke cigarettes.[13]

Due to the complex relationship between family violence and emotional, social, and physical factors, projections for medical training include new curricula to teach staff how to identify domestic violence victims and guide them to resources.[14] Reasons for domestic violence vary, but the patterns of control manifest in predictable ways.

Ultimately, education and support are key to overcoming abuse. One woman's journey to recovery began with a simple handwritten note. She passed it to her physician in the privacy of the examining room during a routine checkup because she didn't know how else to discuss her hurtful situation.

Others will benefit from new medical guidelines desig-nated as preventive measures. Beginning August 2012, the U.S. Department of Health and Human Services will require new health insurance plans to cover domestic violence screening and counseling, without charging a co-payment, co-insurance, or deductible.[15]

While physicians can document medical records in a confi-dential setting, which may later assist victims in court, medical staff must be able to recognize injuries resulting from domestic violence. However, one study showed that only 25 percent of domestic violence victims treated in hospital emergency depart-ments were identified as victims of abuse.[16]

Trauma from domestic violence carries a high emotional and monetary cost. Centers for Disease Control estimated that the medical and other expenses involved with IPV cost more than $5 billion in 2003.[17]

While emergency rooms and shelters house thousands who have been harmed in domestic disputes, many more people cower in the prisons of their homes, hoping that God will some-how offer them relief from verbal and emotional assaults that destroy as surely as physical blows.

Have you suffered due to abuse? If so, know that God doesn't want you to be crippled with terror and confusion. "For you did not receive a spirit that makes you a slave again to fear" (Romans 8:15).

Fear can bind you in bad situations, or fear can send you seeking solutions. How are concerns affecting you today?

In the struggle to make sense of a world gone crazy, enablers often hold back, questioning their own sanity. Abusers use guilt, accuse loved ones of wrongdoing, and point out inadequacies to incapacitate their victims.

Dr. Tian Dayton describes this dynamic in *Emotional Sobriety: From Relationship Trauma to Resilience*, noting, "The codepen-dent person, or the co-addict, was that person who got sick through living with the distorted, unregulated, and out-of-bal-ance thinking, feeling, and behavior that surround addiction."[18]

When you love someone, you tend to get caught up in his or her needs. In a healthy relationship, this looking out for each other is a shared response. However, in dysfunctional arrange-ments, one controlling partner rules absolutely—to the systematic

unhealthy. But worries and a negative outlook keep you pinned to that situation like a bug in a science project display.

When faced with a decision, you freeze in doubt, full of uncertainty. If you leave this individual, can you provide for yourself financially? Will anyone else find you attractive? Who will protect you and care for you? Fear keeps you from making clear decisions and carrying them out.

My early timidity had costly results. Within a few weeks of marriage, Wendell didn't come home one night. As the clock ticked each minute of waiting away, I wondered what happened and if he was OK. A panicked late-night call to his dad revealed Wendell had gone out with his best friend—the one who'd thrown him a seventy-two-hour bachelor party. Most likely, the two of them had embarked on another night of partying and drinking.

I spent the rest of the night agonizing about what to do. At six o'clock the next morning, I packed to go to my parents' house. Wendell arrived as I was leaving and saw the car trunk open, with my suitcase inside. He entered our home and blocked my exit.

Five more minutes and I would have been gone.

Full of anger, I challenged him. "Where have you been? Why didn't you call? I'm sick of you going out drinking!"

He closed the distance between us, put his hands around my throat, and squeezed. The pressure increased until I felt light-headed and saw black spots. *So this is how I'll die*, I thought, looking into Wendell's summer-sky eyes while his grip robbed my breath.

Not once in two years of dating had Wendell physically harmed me. I couldn't believe this was happening.

My knees buckled and he released my throat. Sucking air into my lungs, I thought, *OK, I'm going to be all right*.

Relief didn't last long. Wendell slammed my body onto the couch.

I looked at the keys gripped in my right hand. If I stabbed him to break his hold, could I get away? The thought horrified me because I didn't want to hurt Wendell.

He noticed my gaze and wrenched the key ring from my hand, flinging it across the room. Then he shook me like a rag doll. I struggled, but he was stronger; he battered me until I went limp.

Wendell told me to go to the bedroom. Once there, I looked across the room at the sliding glass doors and imagined running to freedom. But there was no escape. Wendell followed close behind, and I couldn't run fast enough to unlock and open the door.

I complied with his demand for physical intimacy because I didn't want to get hit again. My mind offered the only relief possible: blanking out so the pain and betrayal from someone I loved didn't register.

At the time, I didn't think about asking God to intervene because I felt the Lord had given up on me, leaving me with the consequences of my rebellion.

I wish I had known then that God never wants any of his children to be beaten or belittled. He can redeem all of our mistakes.

In retrospect, I believe that one of the worst aspects of domestic violence is a twisted sense of loyalty to the abuser. You think hiding the problem will prevent other people from knowing. You are ashamed and hope that the current crisis will go away with no further incidents. You make excuses and try to rationalize reasons for why your loved one acted crazy.

The truth is, once violence occurs, you change forever. Even if the physical evidence of bruising heals quickly, the emotional scars are deep. Your ability to trust disappears. Acceptance of even one instance of violence becomes tacit approval for more, and a cycle of abuse and manipulation is established that increases in intensity, unless intentional intervention occurs.

Early in my marriage, shock and grief overwhelmed me. I didn't know what to do. When Wendell's rage cooled by the afternoon, he let me walk outside to get my stuff from the still-open trunk, but he kept the car keys. I didn't have access to cash or a phone to call for help.

In addition to losing any sense of personal safety, I also endured more humiliation. Neighbors from the adjacent duplex stood in their yard. They glanced at me, then looked away. They had to have heard the ruckus that morning through the thin walls, but they said nothing.

Neither did I; I certainly wasn't going to ask the neighbors, "By the way, did you hear my husband beating me this morning after he came home drunk?" Their silence reinforced my shame and sense of rejection.

Thinking I could tough it out and find a way to fix the problem, I sought guidance a few days later from a psychologist, whose office I'd noticed on the way to work.

When I recounted the details of my abuse to this young woman, she looked at me with horror. I felt dirty and guilty, as though I had done something wrong. She didn't offer comfort, advice, or any resources. Her aloofness made it hard to concentrate on anything she said, so I left the session feeling stupid and worthless.

Perhaps she had no training in domestic violence since this issue had yet to garner much public awareness. Virginia didn't create state laws against marital rape and sexual assault until 1986—two years *after* my honeymoon horror.[21]

After the initial abuse as a young bride, I came to two conclusions: nobody cared, and I shouldn't tell anyone. Those beliefs were reinforced at the end of the week when I went to a pool party with Wendell's family, who lived in the area. In silent mutiny, I wore my swimsuit, which clearly revealed large teal and yellow bruises.

"Lydia, those marks look horrible," Wendell's older sister said. "How did you get them?"

"Why don't you ask Wendell?"

She took a furtive glance over her shoulder, then walked away. She never did ask Wendell.

Something died in me that day. I accepted my husband's violence as the consequence for my failure to honor God's law to remain pure before marriage.

All I could do was try to make the best of the situation. I knew of no resources such as shelters for abused women or local meetings of Al-Anon or CoDA.

Uninformed, I didn't know that battering is defined as harm in the form of any physical, emotional, sexual, economic or other behavior designed to assert control and power.[22] In addition to the obvious example of hitting, battering can range from locking you out of your home, to abandoning you in a dangerous place, to refusing to care for you when you're injured.[23]

After that traumatic morning with Wendell, my heart was wounded and I had no spiritual counselor in whom to confide. Besides, I figured if God really cared, he would have protected me. No, God didn't love me, and neither did anyone else. With that bitter attitude, I mired myself in the mindset of a helpless victim and ignored responsibility for my decisions.

I wish I had known then that I had the ability to improve the situation; in fact, that is something we are all capable of, if only we can find the strength.

If you feel powerless, try to remember that things can change, and you have the ability to change them. Take heart and ask God to show you what you can do with his strength. Face your fears and take action to rediscover yourself.

You are a wonderful and amazing person who deserves peace, safety, and contentment. These are within reach when you are ready to stretch your hands out to receive them.

Healing Practice #1: Admit to yourself that a problem exists.

Coming out of hiding requires courage. Once violence begins, whether emotional or physical, the pattern doesn't stop without specific, concentrated intervention.

Study Questions

1. Have you faced a crisis lately? What fears ran through your mind? Write these down and organize the main concerns. For example, are you afraid of being alone? Is money a problem? Do you feel safe?

2. Evaluate your relationship. Are there instances of upheaval, such as harsh words, hostility, or violence? If so, can you recognize a pattern, such as conflict-courtship–complacency, then the whole cycle repeating?

3. Have you stifled your feelings to maintain a routine?

4. Do you spend more energy taking care of other people than of yourself?

5. "The codependent person, or the co-addict, was that person who got sick through living with the distorted, unregulated, and out-of-balance thinking, feeling, and behavior that surround addiction." Does Dr. Dayton's definition describe you? If so, how?

6. Do you have ongoing medical problems, such as stomach pains or headaches? Your body may be trying to signal that you need to attend to underlying emotional issues.

Resources

The National Domestic Violence Hotline is 1-800-799-7233; calls are taken seven days a week, twenty-four hours a day. If you can work from a secure computer, check out the website, http://www.thehotline.org/is-this-abuse/am-i-being-abused-2/.

Help for battered men can be found at http://www.batteredmen.com/ or from WebMD at http://www.webmd.com/balance/features/help-for-battered-men.

Al-Anon is an organization for people who have loved ones who are addicts. It is dedicated to helping people who feel hopeless and have difficulty believing things can ever change for them. In Al-Anon and Alateen, members share their experiences, strength, and hope to learn a better way of life and to find happiness, whether the alcoholic in the family is still drinking or not. For more information, go to http://www.al-anon.alateen. org/meetings/meeting.html, or call 1-888-425-2666 for meeting information in Canada and the United States.

Many people use alcohol to escape inner pain. For more information, contact Alcoholics Anonymous (AA) at P.O. Box 459, New York, NY 10163 or call 212-870-3400. The website, http://www.aa.org/?Media=PlayFlash, has resources, as well as a direc- tory for meetings across the country. The program emphasizes respect for anonymity and teaches steps for recovery.

For information about state alliances against domestic vio- lence funded through the Centers for Disease Control and Prevention, write 4770 Buford Highway NE, Mail Stop F64, Atlanta, GA 30341, phone 1-800-CDC-INFO (232-4636), or e-mail cdcinfo@ cdc.gov. The website is www.cdc.gov/injury.

Sponsored by the federal government, the National Institute on Alcohol Abuse and Alcoholism (NIAAA) publishes easy-to-read, informative online articles about ongoing issues and research surrounding alcoholism. For more information, go to http://www. spectrum.niaaa.nih.gov/default.aspxoffers. The agency also can be contacted at 5635 Fishers Lane, MSC 9304, Bethesda, MD 20892-9304. Communications/Public Information can be reached at 301-443-3860.

CHAPTER | TWO

ISOLATION

*I*n addition to loss of self and fearfulness, another characteristic of the drowning stage is finding yourself isolated from everyone but your partner. You drift away from people strong enough to help you identify and resolve problems. Clinging to your partner is easier than handling a conversation about what really is going on in your life.

In my case, since I had failed to enlist aid from the neighbors, the psychologist, or Wendell's family, I assumed no one else would care. My mistake was seeking assistance from people who weren't qualified or trained to deal with the complexity of domestic violence and alcoholism.

Embarrassment and pride prevented me from talking with my family about being battered. I feared they would say, "We tried to tell you there'd be problems."

My parents had expressed concerns about Wendell before we got married, but I had refused to listen. Therefore, I felt that I couldn't involve them in my mess.

I had tried to discuss the episode with Wendell a few days after the incident, once things had simmered down. "Have you ever done anything like this before?"

"Yes," he said, "with my old girlfriend, but she liked it when I got rough with her."

His response left me speechless.

I didn't bring up the topic again; I was too scared. He didn't either. It was as though the abuse never happened.

That's when the isolation began. I stopped trying to find help and hid within myself. I stuffed that terrible secret of Wendell's cruelty in a tightly locked closet and threw away the key.

Someone who's never experienced violence might wonder why I didn't leave, but the answer to that question isn't simple.

Abuse shatters your spirit. Imagine a fine car parked in a garage. Without warning, someone takes a sledgehammer to the vehicle, bashing in the hood, windows, and windshield. Shards of glass fly everywhere. The tires get slashed.

You certainly can't jump in that vehicle and go. Before you can drive off, you have to make repairs. People who have suffered abuse also need time to recover and heal from shock.

Anxiety and confusion are common reactions to sexual trauma. Other effects can include emotional detachment, sleeping problems, and flashbacks. Studies indicate that victims may show elevated symptoms of stress two years after a rape.[24]

The task of surviving in an environment of constant threat is monumental, particularly as isolation, which signals codependency, limits your access to potential sources of help.

Since I didn't know what else to do, I slipped into a routine where I went to work, keeping a distance from others in the office. Then I went home to Wendell, or waited alone at the house for him to return from a night out with friends. Who would want to be with a loser like me, anyhow?

Like a prisoner of war, I bonded with my captor-husband and assumed my inability to please Wendell was the problem. I still loved him. All I had to do to prevent future problems was be careful not to make him angry. I vowed to be a better wife.

The rationalization to exist in an awful situation can be explained with psychology. Stockholm syndrome is a condition in which victims attach emotionally to abusers as a survival tool.[25] The term originated after a bank robbery in Stockholm, Sweden, when two female hostages continued relationships after their release with the male robbers who had held them captive for several days. One woman became engaged to her former captor, while another raised funds for the robbers' legal defense.

If you have been abused—either physically or verbally—you know how that experience destroys your self-esteem. Juggling each day to avoid more crises consumes all your emotional energy. You tiptoe around, being careful not to anger the abuser again. So much effort goes into dodging trouble that you have nothing left to try to secure yourself.

You exist in a make-believe world with the abuser at the center, allowing yourself to grow smaller and smaller, like a speck of dust floating away.

I realize now that I acted more like a puppy than a person. Eager to please Wendell, I gratefully accepted any tidbit of affection. I became more and more dependent on him, allowing him to hold an intellectual leash that limited my freedom in exchange for the small security of belonging to him.

Bypassing a prime job offer in a respected marketing firm, I chose to accompany Wendell when he took a military assignment a few months after we married. We moved three states away and made a new start. Although Wendell still drank heavily, camouflaging his problem under a military culture that promoted weekends socializing at the club, at least there was no more physical violence. Things seemed to improve with Wendell's steady employment. Two years later, our first child, Steve, was born.

The birth of our son marked a sweet era of closeness. Whenever Steve got fussy, Wendell would put him in the baby swing right by the old piano in the family room. Then Wendell would sit on the bench and play soft tunes until Steve settled down. I loved watching our baby turn toward the sound of the music as Wendell's hands gently touched the keyboard.

Although we had good times, difficulties resurfaced when we decided to leave the military. Economic insecurity haunted us again, but we struggled to keep the marriage going because we cared about each other and had a child to raise.

In our first nine years of marriage, we moved ten times. Each change to facilitate Wendell's professional goals diminished my ability to pursue my dreams. I traveled across five states and gave up friends and family—each time attempting a brave new start to find another job and join a social network.

Giving higher priority to a spouse's goals and dreams is something victims of domestic violence often do. Do you find yourself doing this? If so, why? What strategies do you have for adjusting to upheaval?

Think about relationships you have outside your marriage. What activities do you participate in for recreation? If you have no outlets for your own enjoyment, consider what you can do to pursue your interests. Explore ways you can socialize with others and develop stronger fellowship. Chatting with neighbors and saying hello to someone beside you in the grocery store can be small beginnings to connecting with others around you and lessening your feelings of isolation.

Establishing social connections is a strategy that did provide me with some comfort. Hungering for more out of life and taking to heart my new role as mother, I began seeking God and joined a church. I invited God back into my life, but kept him at arm's length. My relationship with the Lord resembled my first slow dance in junior high school: I stood with my arms held up stiffly and feet shuffling in tiny, awkward circles.

While I was experiencing the beginning of my spiritual awakening, Wendell still struggled with alcohol-related temptations, which led him to go out with friends and get drunk. He shrugged off these occasional breakdowns without apology.

He made it to work every day and had no formal indication of an addiction, such as an arrest. He said I nagged too much, and I questioned my own judgment; maybe Wendell didn't have a problem and I just overreacted.

A gentleman named Clay, with twenty-one years of sobriety through the AA fellowship, explained alcoholism this way: "We start on the process of addiction innocently enough. We don't know one or two drinks will ignite a fire within us that becomes uncontrollable. We aren't thinking that anything bad will happen."

He added, "Eventually, our drinking turns on us and we're addicted. It happens in such a subtle way we didn't even know it."

Living with an alcoholic or addict can be compared with someone accidentally dropping a burnt match on the family room floor. No one notices right away. Soon, you catch a faint smell of smoke, but you aren't sure of the source. Your partner tells you not to worry. You think your mind is playing tricks on you.

With time, embers from the small cinder spread. Eventually, an acrid cloud fills the family room. You close the door to that part of the house because the smoke makes your eyes water. You don't leave the residence because you think you can put out the flames. You get the hose and squirt water on the doorway to dampen the heat. Then you focus on something else.

When you finally realize a blazing inferno is devouring your whole house, you are surprised, wondering how in the world it happened.

On the surface, Wendell appeared to function well, but the emotional toll grew as conversation and intimacy dwindled. Our relationship wasn't good, but it wasn't rotten either. I fantasized that another baby could restore the spark of joy that Wendell and I missed.

I got pregnant again. While I felt delight, Wendell reacted to the added responsibility by spending more time away from home. Unable to face the many pressures, he escaped by working long hours, then spending late nights at a bar with friends. Meanwhile, I felt more isolated at home, tending our toddler and fighting nausea. I felt an incredible loneliness and sorrow. Why couldn't we find happiness?

One oft-quoted definition of insanity is doing the same thing and expecting different results. I found myself trapped in a mental vise where I knew things weren't healthy, but I didn't feel capable of doing anything about it. What could I do when I had a small child counting on me and another baby on the way?

Pointing fingers at Wendell's flaws, I shielded myself from hard looks at what I contributed to the problems, all the while simmering with resentment.

I kept thinking that if only Wendell would take responsibility and not drink, our lives would be fine. I gave him all the power, which only made his burden heavier.

My strategies to get him to stop drinking included giving him the silent treatment and trying to limit his alcohol intake. Sometimes, I'd hide his bottles.

The one thing I didn't do was address why I felt responsible and constantly covered for him. Had I been honest with myself, I would have admitted that managing Wendell meant I didn't have to look at my own emptiness.

For one couple I knew, alcoholism jeopardized everything they held dear. The housewife's alcohol addiction grew to where her husband feared for the safety of their young children while he was away at work. In desperation, he called police one morning on the way to his job and asked them to check on his family. When police arrived at the home, they did a Breathalyzer test on the wife. Her blood-alcohol level registered one-and-a-half times more than the legal limit for intoxication.[26] Officers transported her to jail at nine o'clock that morning.

The wife, too lost in her own needs, later told me how angry she was about spending time in a cell because no one posted her bail. She couldn't see the tragic risk she posed to the children. She told me, "I'd only sipped one drink and I was fine. I don't know why everyone overreacted."

Crisis Forces a Decision

Addictions will continue to result in the deterioration of your loved one—and you—if problems aren't addressed. Brief periods of calm may exist, but sooner or later there will be another crisis. Don't let the relative quiet lull you into complacency like it did me.

When Steve was two years old and Luke, our second son, was a few months old, Wendell came home late and drunk—again. Exhausted from child-rearing responsibilities and irate about his behavior, I yelled at him. He shoved me up against the cabinets in the den, but I managed to twist away and fled outside the house.

A few minutes later, I tried to go back for the children, but Wendell had locked me out. In this emergency, my faith took on a new intensity. *Lord God, please protect my babies!*

With no shoes, purse, or keys, I ran to the neighbor's place and asked to borrow her phone. She welcomed me in without flinching at my disheveled appearance.

I didn't want to call the police with my neighbor listening; I wanted to protect Wendell's reputation. Besides, Wendell was the breadwinner of our family, so I phoned Wendell's friend Kyle.

"Hey, this is Lydia. Could you come over right away? I'm locked out of the house."

Kyle arrived in minutes—perhaps he heard the undertones of terror in my voice. He climbed the second-story deck and found a balcony door unlocked.

While waiting for him to let me inside, I looked through a window and saw Wendell asleep on a bed in the basement.

"Do you want me to go in with you?" Kyle asked after opening the front door.

"No. I'll be all right."

After thanking Kyle for coming to my rescue, I rushed into the house and went to check on the boys. They weren't in their upstairs bedroom, where I'd left them. After searching the house in quiet desperation, I tiptoed to the basement bedroom, where Wendell snored. The boys' little bodies were curled up beside him like prizes in his lair.

Holding my breath as I lifted each son, I prayed the shift in weight wouldn't alert Wendell. He snorted in his drunken stupor but turned over without waking.

What if Wendell had rolled over on the children and hurt them? Something had to be done.

After relocating the boys upstairs, I spent the rest of the night trying to figure out what to do. This second instance of physical violence, even though it occurred six years after the first battering, foreshadowed a pattern I couldn't allow.

My tentative faith in God's love had grown to the point where I saw his hand in the boys' protection that night. I asked for his help in knowing what to do.

Ignoring the problem of Wendell's alcoholism wasn't going to work anymore. This crisis affecting my boys galvanized me to take action, and the first step was to face my pride. To get help, I'd have to humble myself and disclose my need, something I had been reluctant to do. But there was no way around that if I was going to keep my family safe.

In the morning, after Wendell went to work, I phoned my mother and asked to borrow money. I hoped she wouldn't ask questions, and luckily, she didn't.

A girlfriend offered to babysit while I met with an attorney to find out about filing a restraining order.

"You can go to the courthouse and fill out the form yourself," the attorney said. "That'll be the cheapest way."

Once again, I felt rejected by a professional whose help I had sought in an emergency. Couldn't the lawyer see my fear? Yet I felt God whisper to my heart that he would sustain me.

My problem had escalated beyond what I could tolerate. I had experienced Wendell's pummeling once, and I had no intention of ever being hurt like that again, particularly with our sons at risk. I hoped that going public with our horrible family secret would require an accountability of Wendell, at last.

At the courthouse, tears blurred my vision as I strained to complete the paperwork. How could I betray my husband like this? Would he ever forgive me? But a louder voice in my head replied, *How can you let Wendell endanger you and your children?*

I had justified the first incident of domestic violence as my price for poor choices, but my maternal instinct would not allow the boys' well-being to be jeopardized.

After picking up the children from my friend's house, I went home and started packing. I didn't know exactly what to do, but I knew I had to do something.

If you find yourself in a similar situation, you need an exit plan, and this involves preparation to ensure your safety. Suggestions include: set aside cash you can use in an emergency; store a few clothing items with friends or neighbors; keep spare keys in a spot known only to you; have a list of important phone numbers and addresses with you at all times; and keep legal records, such as a Social Security card, driver's license, and birth certificate, close at hand.[27]

Because cell phones can be tracked, consider getting a separate, prepaid one for yourself. Program 9-1-1 in this phone for any emergency. Also, you need to be aware that any research you do on your home computer can be found, even after you delete your browser history. Consider instead doing your investigations at public libraries or a friend's house.

I had no background in this kind of planning during my difficulties; I made do as best as I could, grabbing diapers and extra baby bottles. The boys and I would need to stay some-where else until the deputy served notice. Wendell usually fin-ished work around five o'clock, and I planned to leave the house long before then. At three o'clock, his truck pulled in the driveway.

Wendell picked up on my nervous pacing and idle chatter. "What's going on?"

I confessed requesting a restraining order. "A deputy will be here around five o'clock."

"Call them and cancel," he demanded.

I phoned the dispatcher to defuse the situation while Wendell glared at me, but she couldn't stop the order. "You'll have to talk with the deputy when he gets there," she said.

In this precarious situation, would Wendell become enraged and attack me? My stomach knotted with anxiety.

I think what saved me was that Wendell knew he couldn't do anything without authorities finding out. Not only had I completed paperwork at the courthouse, but a dispatcher had recorded the call, and a deputy would be arriving soon.

My unexpected assertiveness caught Wendell off guard and shifted power from him to me. During the wait for the deputy, Wendell begged for my forgiveness. I wanted to believe him, but how could I be sure the boys and I would be safe? I felt confused. Didn't God want me to be a faithful wife?

Soon after five, a knock at the front door signaled the dep-uty's arrival. Surprised to see a female officer alone, I invited her inside. Showing great compassion, she talked with us for an hour, encouraging us to get help from an organization like AA or through family counseling.

"You know, alcoholism causes problems in a lot of families," she said in a soft tone.

With a bowed head, Wendell received her kind advice with humility. I couldn't tell if it was because he really felt sorry for what he'd done or if he needed to impress an authority figure.

What I did know was that I would never again allow myself be attacked like I had after the honeymoon. This awakening to my own power felt good.

Remember that many people—my neighbor, Mom, Wendell's friend Kyle, the employees at the courthouse, and the deputy—all readily supported me when I made known exactly what I needed. You will find the same to be true in your time of need; just keep your eyes open and be willing to ask. Decide what you want and choose when to take definite action. Come up with a strategy that works for you and meets your requirements.

Resolve Dwindles as the Crisis Fades

Believing God had intervened by sending us an angel in the form of a wise, caring deputy, I thought we had a second chance to heal our marriage. Wendell and I worked at reconciliation, and he promised he wouldn't drink again.

Soon after the crisis, I visited a support group meeting but couldn't relate to the other people. I shortchanged myself by limiting my exposure to one trip.

Deciding Wendell needed to take the lead, I settled back into my mental cocoon of "this is his problem," and I went about my life as before, tending the children and keeping house.

I got lazy and failed to continue exercising my newfound power. Without an immediate threat, sustaining the energy to demand change required too much effort. Besides, Wendell promised he'd behave.

Rather than set my own goals, I continued to ride on Wendell's railroad tracks. I supported his decisions, not allowing myself to think too much about how fragile our peace was.

A similar experience is recounted by a woman named Betty; she, too, recognized that the relationship rules with her husband needed to change, but she didn't press forward. Indecision immobilized her. "Why didn't I see what was coming?" she later mourned. "Why didn't I prepare? It was like I fell asleep at the wheel and didn't know what I woke up to."

Is this something you can relate to? Have you made a stand, only to let the ground you gained disappear? Do you make tough declarations but fail to enforce them? How might inconsistency ruin your ability to impact the relationship in positive ways?

In my case, I had developed a false sense of security; I believed that his knowing I would take legal action would keep Wendell in check. We tried to repair our relationship. We made enough progress that when Wendell took another job out of state, I felt comfortable going with him and taking our sons.

We moved a thirteen-hour drive away from anyone we knew. For the first time, we joined a church together and worked to become part of a new community. With my parents' help, we bought an older house. Wendell demonstrated his love by laboring to restore and beautify the structure. He hammered, sawed, and painted to rebuild.

The reconstruction of our lives progressed, and we had a few golden years. But Wendell didn't seek outside help, and neither did I. We thought we could handle the situation ourselves, but we were wrong.

The number of people dependent on alcohol who seek help is low—only 15 percent.[28] Without a support system and treatment, few heavy drinkers can sustain abstinence from alcohol for long. All their good intentions collapse the next time a major stressor occurs.

After a few years of stability, Wendell got fired. The problems we'd hidden soon resurfaced.

"I'm going to start my own business," he said. "You need to be my secretary."

"I don't want to be a secretary," I responded.

Wendell clenched his jaw as his face flushed red. "If you don't want to help, get out."

The old specter of abandonment reared its ugly head again. I couldn't support myself and the boys, and I wasn't about to leave our sons or move in with my parents, so I backed down. But I made a silent vow never to be in such a helpless position again. Economic dependence and fear had kept me hostage too long.

A few months after Wendell's threat to force me out of our home, he said he wanted us to have another baby. But this time around, I knew better than to believe a child could heal the rifts in our marriage. I certainly didn't feel safe enough to be completely dependent with another infant to nurture. I told Wendell that I couldn't continue to home-school our sons while caring for a new baby. Because Wendell loved our sons and wanted them to have the best, he honored my decision not to have another child.

In control of my body and free to seek a new direction, I used the fear of being kicked out of my own home to forge my half-hearted commitments about change into a burning desire for more options. I finally felt ready to take serious action.

A friend from church helped me get a part-time job teaching at a middle school, and I enrolled in a local college to complete a program for a teaching license. I began moving out in independent ways, trusting God to lead me through the changes.

Learning to trust my own judgment helped me tap into talents I'd allowed to lie dormant. After a couple of years working part time and going to school, I graduated with honors and a degree in education. Then I accepted an offer for a full-time teaching position at the high school Steve would enter as a freshman.

As I gradually took more responsibility for myself, I felt freer and happier than I had in a long time. My mind-set changed from seeing obstacles to imagining possibilities.

Wendell noticed my determination and treated me with more respect. He applauded my efforts, sending me flowers at school on my first day of work with a card that read, "Congratulations on achieving your dream."

I enjoyed feeling like a partner, rather than a dependent. Each little success bred hope in me that I could accomplish even more.

Steering the course of my own life was empowering for me, as it can be for you; all you have to do is take the reins. No matter what mistakes you have made in the past, God invites you to see a good future, one in which he'll develop your talents. All he asks of you is to show the resolve to explore options. He will stay by your side to guide you to a better place.

Healing Practice #2: If you want change to occur, take action.

Within you is a reservoir of strength that empowers you to break patterns of abuse. If you are willing to try, God will show you what steps to take.

Study Questions

1. Do you wait around for someone else to make the changes needed? What would you like to be different?

2. Do you often feel helpless? Why? What measures can you begin today to establish yourself on more solid footing?

3. When was the last time you let God know what you needed and asked for his help?

4. Be alert this week to new opportunities that God may provide for you. Just as my friend helped me find a job, the Lord will lead you to resources. The main question is not whether the Lord will help; the issue is whether you will embrace a chance to better your situation.

5. Write down a list of resources available to you (for example, job potential, skills demonstrated with hobbies, savings accounts, personal possessions, network of friends and acquaintances, public facilities such as libraries and mass transit). How can you use these connections more fully to expand yourself?

Resources

A tremendous book about setting healthy limits is *Boundaries: When to Say Yes, When to Say No, to Take Control of Your Life* by Dr. Henry Cloud and Dr. John Townsend (Zondervan 1992).

Stephen Ministries (http://www.stephenministries.org/) is a group of trained laypersons that offers confidential, Christian support for people experiencing crises. Services are offered free of charge.

Not to People Like Us: Hidden Abuse in Upscale Marriages by Susan Weitzman (Basic Books 2000) explores case studies of women she counseled who came from wealthy backgrounds but still endured domestic violence. Dr. Weitzman discusses tactics used by abusers to manipulate and strategies that victims employed to find healing.

Emerge is a Massachusetts-based organization to help eliminate violence in intimate relationships. Emerge seeks to educate individual abusers and prevent young people from learning to accept violence in their relationships. Resources can be found at http://www.emergedv.com/ or by writing 2464 Massachusetts Avenue, Suite 101, Cambridge, MA 02140. The main office number is 617-547-9879 or fax 617-547-0904.

CHAPTER THREE

Counting Costs

*Y*ou might be thinking that you'd love to make changes, but you can't afford to talk with a lawyer or go to school. You don't know anyone who could help you pay for the expenses involved with change. The whole idea of having options seems impossible. Be encouraged that many local and regional agencies can, and will, assist you in finding a way out of your dilemma.

There is an upsurge in public awareness about the need to improve services for victims of domestic abuse. At the national level, a nonprofit women's advocacy group partnered in a 2009 petition to the Supreme Court to hear a case about privacy and safety concerns for a victim of domestic violence.[29] This appeal captures the complexity of issues surrounding domestic cases.

The scenario began when a woman contacted domestic advocacy services for protection from her former partner. Soon afterward, this man came to her home, refused to leave and became abusive and threatening. Police issued a trespass notice keeping him from coming to her apartment. When the woman informed her landlord about the situation, the landlord asked her to vacate the premises within a few days.[30]

Not only was the woman harassed by her former partner, but now she faced an adversarial relationship with her landlord. When the woman refused to leave, the landlord filed charges against her. The woman's lawyer became involved. The landlord and woman eventually settled their differences.

However, when the woman asked the court to remove her full name from records regarding the settled incident, officials denied her request. Even though the litigation wasn't her fault, the woman feared she might not be able to secure future housing from other landlords.

While some victims wrestle with the court system to find justice, others rely on government assistance to protect them. The U.S. Department of Justice funds an Office for Victims of Crime, which compiles an online directory of organizations that assist victims of domestic abuse. Services range from offering housing to providing legal advocacy, financial aid, and counseling. The Centers for Disease Control and Prevention also distributes federal funds to support state coalitions working to prevent domestic violence.

Learning about these resources can seem intimidating at first, but can you afford not to research options? The potential to ensure your safety is well worth the risk of time spent investigating.

As long as your partner is in active addiction, you cannot count on him or her to have the clarity to know how to improve the situation in your household. It is up to you to take steps and access resources. Your life may depend on your willingness to learn and grow.

Change can be uncomfortable, but it doesn't have to be bad; sometimes, the very thing you resist is what you benefit from the most.

My willingness to go back to school resulted in a new job that would give me financial security and independence. While I made positive strides forward, Wendell floundered. He couldn't make his business profitable. Rather than seek advice, he tried to escape with a geographic solution by taking a job back in the state where we grew up. Since I'd already signed a teaching contract and we owned a house, this presented another dilemma. Would I give up everything again to follow him? Or would I make a stand on my own?

Completing the education program and finishing a successful teaching internship gave me confidence that I could manage without Wendell. The boys liked their schools and didn't want to lose their friends, and that gave me a good excuse for choosing a new path, one in which I stepped up to assume financial and emotional leadership. The boys and I held the fort at home, settled into a routine, and looked forward to Wendell's visits.

But the long-distance separation presented difficulties. We didn't get to see each other often because plane tickets were expensive. Wendell couldn't attend many of the boys' sporting events, and I had all the day-to-day parenting responsibilities.

Without my steady presence, Wendell made different lifestyle choices. Once, when I visited his out-of-state apartment, I found his pantry full of half-empty bottles of hard liquor. When I asked him that night after work why he stocked so much alcohol, he said, "I only promised you that I wouldn't drink in our home. This apartment doesn't count."

I lacked the energy to take definite action. After all, he was already gone; what else could I demand? He was an adult who had to make his own decisions. I couldn't control him and no longer wanted to try, particularly since I had a safe place separate from him and had proven my ability to provide for myself and the boys.

Over time, Wendell's trips home became less frequent, down to a day or two every five or six weeks. I tried to be understanding, but the divide between us kept widening. After a year of this seesawing, I called him. The unclear state of our marriage needed to be addressed; I had been patient long enough.

"Wendell, your sons need a father, and I need a husband. Come back home or we'll have to establish official separation. We're living apart anyhow."

He must have heard the certainty and finality in my tone. Wendell gave up his job and moved back with us. But he wasn't happy about the ultimatum, particularly since he couldn't find another job. While he struggled to establish himself, I kept busy teaching school and volunteering at church.

Making a Stand

Alcoholism is sneaky. Once an addiction takes hold—and no one knows exactly when the enjoyment of alcohol crosses over into dependency—the amount of alcohol required to sustain the abuser's level of satisfaction must increase. This biological and emotional demand takes precedence over everything else.

The alcoholic often becomes numb to anything but the need for a buzz that he or she is oblivious to how the addiction destroys everyone in the family. Craving relief from the pain inside them, alcoholics are blind to everything except when they'll get their next drink.

This proved true for Wendell. While I felt glad he was home, I had completely underestimated the control his addiction now exerted over him. I'd be up one day with hope that things would improve, then down the next because nothing ever seemed to change. A few weeks before Valentine's Day—three months before our twentieth anniversary—Wendell traveled back to his old job for weekend duty. At three o'clock Saturday morning, the bedside phone startled me awake. Before I could grab it, the answering machine recorded a woman talking, while Wendell's slurred voice made comments in the background.

Now I understood Wendell's preference to live and work out of state: he must be involved with another woman. This knowledge hurt terribly, but it also provided a strange relief. Finally, there was proof of a real problem and not just my vague notion that alcohol poisoned us all.

I called Wendell's office around seven o'clock, leaving a cryptic message about a family emergency.

Wendell phoned several hours later. "I heard you needed me. What's going on?"

"Why was a strange woman talking on the phone with you at three this morning?"

After a slight hesitation, he said, "Must have been a wrong number."

"I heard your voice in the background. The answering machine recorded it."

"Oh." He paused again, then started talking rapidly. "Must have happened at the party last night. I had to drive a coworker and his wife home because they'd been drinking."

That sounded plausible. But something still didn't feel right.

"So you won't mind if I call them to confirm?"

How did I have the composure to say that?

It turned out that Wendell's alibi was a lie. I felt sick. Although I'd put up with physical violence and years of financial upheaval, I drew the line at unfaithfulness.

Oddly enough, even with Wendell's deceit confirmed, I held on to hope. Wasn't love all about forgiveness? Didn't I have to work things out for our sons?

I also battled fear. Perhaps I was unworthy of anything better.

When our teenage sons woke up, I told them about the phone call. I figured they were mature enough to handle the truth and deserved to be prepared for what might unfold.

Wendell took the first flight out and returned home that afternoon; he seemed eager to work on the marriage. Although he swore infidelity hadn't occurred, he never apologized for lying. Within a week, Wendell planned a family vacation for all of us to a Caribbean island.

"Baby, I promise you I won't drink alcohol anymore," Wendell said.

I breathed a sigh of relief. We could only move forward if he stayed sober. I also demanded that he provide a medical report proving he had no sexually transmitted diseases, and he complied.

The vacation felt awkward. Bad weather outside mirrored tensions in the rental house where we were cooped up. Although there was no drinking or violence, the lack of emotional closeness forced me to see the emptiness of our marriage.

After the holiday, neither Wendell nor I sought outside help, such as a family counselor. We didn't involve our church family in the sordid circumstances—that would have been embarrassing.

I confided in a few close friends. Although they tried to comfort me, they weren't able to advise me on how to improve things. How much more would I have to take before I realized my continued optimism and loyalty were foolish?

How do you know when your faithfulness to your spouse actually enables inappropriate behavior? Can you define clear limits of what you'll stand? Or do you continue to make excuses, too frightened to face the cost of implementing change?

Holding the Bag
One Time Too Many

If you're like me, you try to manage the craziness swirling around you. You aren't certain that things will ever be right, but you are reluctant to let go because you've already invested too much in making the marriage work. You value family and will do whatever it takes to keep your loved ones together.

Wendell and I had weathered another storm, but I felt uneasy. The dilemma about what to do puzzled me. I wanted to trust Wendell and believe we could pull through, but the many instances of upheaval over the years had taught me to be cautious.

I asked God what I should do, but he seemed to remain silent. I tried to pick up the pieces and adjust to having Wendell home.

Wendell insulated himself from me with a steady flow of his family and friends as houseguests. I felt more like a hotel manager than a wife. We settled into mindless routines for several months. But one night early in November, neither of us could sleep.

"I've lost hope that our marriage can heal," I whispered to him in our dark, cold bed.

Wendell cajoled me into believing the marriage could work, saying, "Honey, you know I love you."

Then he pushed for physical intimacy, and I wearily agreed, just like I had in college. Maybe my aloofness caused our problems. I should try to please him. In my mind an old tape played that if only I worked harder, things would improve.

I arose at five the next morning to get ready to teach, though I hadn't slept much. Fatigue made the day pass slowly. Driving home, I anticipated a few hours of rest before more company arrived that evening. When I walked in the house at four o'clock, fourteen-year-old Luke met me.

"Mom, you've got to take me to the emergency room," he wheezed.

His tears got my attention. This six-foot-tall, 160-pound basketball player hadn't shed a tear when his shoulder broke during a game. His face was pale but there were no signs of illness, other than the strained breathing.

"Let's go."

I set the papers I had to grade on the kitchen counter and turned toward seventeen-year-old Steve. "Wait here, in case the relatives arrive before Dad gets home from work."

Steve nodded. I put my arm around Luke's shoulders and we walked to the car. Luke hunched over in his seat while I drove. At a stop light, I reached over with my hand, pressing the inside of my wrist against his forehead. It felt hot.

"Do you have pain in any specific spot?"

"I hurt all over," he mumbled.

In the crowded emergency room, Luke shivered as we waited. After two hours, we got a room and a doctor entered to examine Luke.

After listening to Luke's chest, the physician said, "He might have pneumonia. I'm going to order chest X-rays and start him on IV fluids. I'll get back with you when the results come in."

Soon after the doctor left, a nurse arrived to insert an IV needle into Luke's arm. While she set up the equipment, I went down the hall to the vending machine to get crackers. It had been hours since I'd eaten.

Back in Luke's room, I settled in the chair beside his bed while he dozed. The hospital room phone rang, and I answered.

"What's going on with Luke?" asked Wendell's older sister, one of the relatives expected to arrive that day.

"The doctor thinks he might have pneumonia. We're waiting to get X-rays. That might take a while because the hospital is packed."

"Dad, Brad, and I are starving after driving all day. Wendell is taking us to the buffet. Do you want anything?"

"No, thanks. I just had a snack."

I wanted to ask for a full-course dinner, but for some reason I hesitated. Doubtful about her genuine affection for me after the swimsuit episode years ago, I didn't want to impose. Besides, I was sure she must be tired after the thirteen-hour drive. Still, I hoped Wendell would come to the hospital soon. It was only a few miles from the restaurant.

But Wendell never stopped by; he didn't even call. With each hour of his absence, my anger grew. I had become accustomed to his neglect of me, but how could he ignore our son's need?

Around eleven o'clock, the doctor signed discharge papers. While I walked to the parking garage to get the car, a nurse brought Luke in a wheelchair to the entrance. After seven exhausting hours in the hospital, we got home around midnight.

I helped Luke to his bedroom, then entered the dark kitchen to eat. Finding a package of raisin bread on the counter, I unwrapped the bag and munched on a slice. When I turned to get a glass of water, I saw an almost-empty gallon of wine on the counter.

Did Wendell's relatives bring the bottle or had he used guests as an excuse to bring it home?

Dirty wine glasses sat in the sink, screaming at me about another broken promise. I thought about all the hours I'd spent in the hospital, wishing Wendell were beside me. Now the reason was clear. Having alcohol meant more to him than caring for Luke or me.

After years of excusing, trusting, hoping, and coping, something in me snapped. Just that morning Wendell had assured me of his love and commitment, and now he'd allowed alcohol in our house, against my express wishes.

Rage grew in the pit of my stomach, burning like ice held too long. That wine represented a violation of the one pledge I counted on after the other-woman episode.

My wait-and-see approach, believing Wendell would change, proved useless. I'd squandered many years choosing blindness over reality.

A dam of pent-up emotions burst in me. All the years I'd waited and tried harder broke loose in a torrent of images of betrayal and abandonment by Wendell. I began to see that the cost of implementing change in our marriage might be less expensive than continuing to demean myself.

Grabbing the dirty glasses by the throats, I stomped to the French doors, yanked them open, and marched like an executioner toward the edge of the second-story wood deck. I dropped the burgundy-stained goblets over the railing. Disappointment reigned when no tinkle of shattering glass sounded. But I had declared war, even if no one had yet heard the trumpet.

If you find yourself in a similar situation, I don't know what crisis will spur you to take action, but I pray that some incident will so fire you up that you will cast off the shackles of subservience. Remaining stuck in repeating patterns of neglect damages everyone. God will champion a righteous cause, and your desire for your family to be healthy is a goal that he applauds.

Healing Practice #3: Healthy anger is a tool you can use wisely for self-protection.

Like a red check-engine light on a car's dashboard, anger signals something is amiss. Being alert to this emotion enables you to take appropriate precautions and ensure your safety.

Study Questions

1. Have you ever set a boundary or rule, such as no more alcohol in the house, only to have it violated? What happened? Did anyone use distractions to camouflage the main issue?

2. Have you made do for so long on little or no affection that you don't really expect much from your spouse anymore? Has a gradual tide of neglect eroded any sense that you deserve care and gentle love?

3. Evaluate the history of your marriage. Make two columns on a piece of paper. On one side, write memories of good times. On the other, record the crises, disappointments, and problems. Do any patterns emerge when you look at both columns?

4. Do you have access to wise counselors who can advise you and pray for you? Have you humbled yourself to seek guidance from fair-minded people who have your best interests at heart?

Resources

A good book to help you rediscover yourself is *The Language of Letting Go* by Melody Beattie. The text features daily devotions that highlight healing thoughts and help you clarify goals and direction. Hazelden first published this book in 1990.

Understanding how Christian principles affect marriages with violence is addressed in *Keeping the Faith: Guidance for Christian Women Facing Abuse* by Marie M. Fortune. Copyrighted in 1987, the publisher is HarperSanFrancisco, an imprint of HarperCollins.

CHAPTER FOUR

Awakening Courage

You'll come to a point in your life with an active addict where you must decide how much more you can take. Rest assured that if the alcoholic is not willing to get help or stop consuming, then the situation you find yourself in today is as good as life gets.

That means you get to make a choice. You can go along with things as they are, absorbing more pain and disappointments. You can continue to desperately tread water and gasp for air until you exhaust yourself and find relief slowly sinking under as you lose consciousness.

Or, you can awaken your courage and declare you are not going to take any more nonsense. My friend Dee described it this way: "Enough is enough and too much is nasty!"

But making such a proclamation won't be enough to change the established dysfunctional dynamics in your family. Too many times in the past you gave your loved one an ultimatum, only to get wishy-washy later. This time if you're serious—and have a win-the-war mindset that would make any general proud—then you will mobilize.

"When you live with people who have an addiction, they can turn your head around," said my friend Dianne. "You get tired of putting up with things that you know aren't right. You make a decision and stand firm in it. Then the other person can choose what he or she will do. But if they won't cooperate, they know you're moving on."

This decision to move forward takes guts because there is no guarantee you can bring the addict you love with you to a better place. You are going to have to face the fact that saving yourself might mean leaving the alcoholic behind.

All the self-doubt and hesitation that had blocked my ability to make a decision and stick to it throughout the years disappeared. I wanted to transform my life and decided to trade my role as a shadow person for a full flesh-and-blood one. Believing I could take care of myself and the boys, I now was equally certain that Wendell couldn't be trusted to take care of any of us.

Giving my husband more chances seemed a ridiculous proposition. For me, it became clear that being patient and being stupid were two entirely different things. I prepared to make change happen, having peace of mind that this time, events were not due to any fault of mine.

The next morning, while the household slept, I arose early for work. During my lunch break, I rushed home to check on Luke and give him medicine. When I entered the front door, an eerie quiet greeted me. I thought the house would be bustling with company, but I didn't see a soul.

Upstairs, I found Wendell, dressed in blue jeans, a cotton work shirt, and boots, lying beside Luke on the bed. Both stared at me as I entered the room. Neither smiled or greeted me.

I went to my son and asked, "How are you feeling?"

Luke clenched his teeth and tried to sit up straight. Ignoring my question, he countered in a contemptuous tone, sounding like his father, "What happened to the company?"

"I don't know. I've been gone since six thirty this morning."

Wendell bolted upright. "They left because you're so rude," he shouted. "My sister found the wine glasses she gave us for a wedding present outside in the grass. She called me at the job site, asking if she needed to get a hotel."

He glared at me. "When I got here, they had their bags in the car, with the engine running."

So, his family had evacuated. Apparently that was more important to him than my being in the emergency room for hours. He showed no concern for his sick son.

"You are too volatile and out of control," Wendell snarled. "We need to discuss this. Now." I couldn't believe Wendell's venom, particularly in front of Luke.

Although Wendell never uttered curse words at me, his ominous tone indicated that severe consequences loomed for my behavior. How dare he criticize me when he hadn't cared enough to help at the hospital? I refused to be cowed by his antics.

"You and I will talk after work," I said, concerned about Luke sitting in the middle of the crossfire. "I'm going to give Luke his antibiotics and then I have to go back for class."

Wendell leaned back against the headboard of the bed, moving possessively closer to Luke. Wendell's attack about my lack of hospitality sidetracked any discussion about why alcohol was in the house, and why Wendell hadn't called or helped at the hospital.

A prime strategy of alcoholics when dodging their own inadequacies is to attack you for something. Accused of a shortcoming, you'll grow defensive and fail to follow up on the issue revolving around alcohol. Don't let that strategy derail you. Dodge the cannon of distraction and let the smoke roll by. You stick to your guns and hold that addict accountable, but carefully choose your time and place for a safe confrontation.

Arguing in front of Luke wasn't my idea of responsible parenting, so I disengaged, saying I'd talk with Wendell after work.

That night after dinner, in the privacy of our bedroom, Wendell said, "I want a divorce."

I wanted to feel remorse, but instead, relief glimmered. Having the D-word spoken aloud first by Wendell freed me to see his selfishness.

People with addictions and control issues become so wrapped up in their own needs that they can't see anyone else's. The mistake that codependents make is thinking they must protect and help the abuser. In giving too much, codependents harm themselves, as well as their loved ones.

Only when an abuser experiences consequences can he or she begin to see that a problem exists. When a codependent backs off from assuming all responsibility, then the addict actually has a chance to acknowledge issues.

Changing Mindset

When I stepped back and stopped trying to carry the weight of the world, I began thinking that life without Wendell might be more peaceful. If I had to do all the work myself anyway, why did I need him? The old fears of abandonment didn't resurface. I'd already been living alone emotionally a long time—despite being in a crowded house with Wendell.

I wanted off the merry-go-round marriage as much as he wanted me gone, so I looked my husband straight in the eye and agreed to end the relationship; yet that decision brought no real peace in my heart.

Marital unfaithfulness can be considered biblical grounds for divorce (Matthew 19:9), yet I had no solid proof of Wendell's infidelity from the out-of-state incident just a few months prior. I had tried to forgive him, even for that grievous disloyalty.

Through the night as I tried to sleep, the tension between religious values and reality tore me apart. What would happen to our sons?

I knew the Bible said God hates divorce. But God also warned men not to break faith with their wives. Scripture says God despises "a man's covering himself with violence" (Malachi 2:13–16). Violence consists of more than physical punches; it includes withholding affection, making demeaning comments, destroying another person's confidence, and limiting financial access. I didn't want to disobey God, but I didn't know what else to do to protect myself and the boys. Wendell's complete disregard for how he hurt me destroyed my ability to hope.

Time Wendell had spent away prepared me to exist independently. I figured the boys and I would go on living as we had, and Wendell could move on to whatever made him happy. I'd spent two decades attempting to satisfy him, but I could never do enough, and I was sick of trying.

The next morning, I made an appointment with an attorney to draw up legal papers for a separation based on mutual agreement. This document protected me against a potential claim by Wendell of desertion.

Two days later, Wendell went by the law office to sign the document. That night, we calmly told the boys together. Steve wept, his large body crumpled on the couch. While Wendell hugged Steve, Luke remained stoic. I, too, felt frozen in grief.

During the next two weeks, Wendell and I argued over which of us would find another residence. Suddenly, the house he frequently left became his cherished possession.

Maybe Wendell thought the risk of losing shelter would intimidate me and make me back down, as it had in the past. But I had crossed over from a place of confusion to decision-making. Unknowns in the world caused less fear than what I faced inside the home. I was not safe around Wendell. I needed to find refuge for the kids and me, away from alcoholism and abusive manipulation.

Being safe, physically and emotionally, trumped any nostalgia about remaining in the neighborhood where I'd lived for almost eight years. Besides, I couldn't afford to make the mortgage payment on my modest teaching salary.

After work and on weekends, I visited apartment complexes. One place Steve and I toured had a broken window and a filthy toilet. Part of me considered taking the nasty place as punishment for my failure to make the marriage succeed.

"This place isn't going to work," Steve said. "You need something better."

His affirmation encouraged me. But more fruitless searching and high rental rates caused me to almost despair of being able to find a place.

God, help me, because I can't go back to living like I have been.

"Mom, you've got to look at this as an adventure," Steve counseled when I came home after work dejected that there seemed to be no affordable places.

I thought that was an odd piece of advice from my child. It indicated he didn't expect me to work things out with Wendell. This mature young man didn't plead with me to try to save the marriage, nor did he suggest that I had overreacted to Wendell's offenses. Instead he encouraged me to find creative ways to overcome the obstacles blocking my independence.

Throughout my marriage, one of my main goals had been to secure the relationship so our children would have stability. Over time, however, I realized that living with a spouse in active addiction meant there would be constant upheaval for all of us.

Although my sons never saw physical violence between Wendell and me, they observed Wendell's blatant disrespect for me and the power imbalance between us.

My older son's supportive words allowed me to see that my attempts to hold everything together hadn't fooled the children; they knew things weren't right. Maybe my bold moves now would free them to discuss issues that I had carefully tried to hide.

If you have children, consider talking with them on an age-appropriate level about what they are feeling. Being able to talk helps them make sense of the chaos surrounding them and protects them from believing that problems are their fault.

As many as ten million children are estimated to be exposed to domestic violence each year, with approximately fifteen million children living in homes where IPV happened.[31]

No matter how young, children feel the unspoken tensions and fears in a household that revolves around an alcoholic. The kids learn from your example how to tiptoe around.

A young man in his twenties named Justin described his experience growing up in an alcoholic household: "I never felt carefree," he said. "I was too busy listening for things said—and those things unsaid." Shrugging his shoulders, he added, "I didn't have it as bad as some people, though. I realize that being hypersensitive helps me now because I see a lot in business transactions that others miss."

Children learn how to negotiate and set boundaries by watching you. If you fail to establish respectful limits with your spouse, you leave your children vulnerable in their own relationships. To stop the cycle of abuse for your children, you have to break away from your unhealthy coping patterns.

Gathering Resources

Breaking away from dysfunction means doing things differently, and you'll need to look for new resources that are available to you.

Over time, I had gotten a good job and knew lots of people. Forcing myself to see positives helped me to get past barricades, and there were many.

Wendell didn't offer any financial resources to fund the separation, and I knew better than to ask. He would have said something like, "If you want to break up our family, go ahead, but I'm not going to have that on my conscience." Of course, he would ignore any part he'd played in forcing the arrangement.

According to a national poll, more than 25 percent of the respondents believed the inability to access funds for support prevented victims from leaving abusers.[32]

I considered my options. I could live with a single girlfriend down the street or sublet someone's basement. But I needed a place where the boys, our retrievers, and I would feel comfortable. I wanted a haven that offered long-term respite from Wendell's pressure.

Several years earlier, my parents had given me bank stocks. I'd never considered touching them because I wanted to use them toward college for the boys. However, I decided the money might be better spent to secure safe housing. After talking privately with the boys, I made the decision to sell some of the stocks. I figured the money could go back into the college fund when Wendell paid me my half of our home's value.

With a down payment, I could afford a decent house, and the monthly cost would be less than paying rent. Gratitude flooded me as I realized that God had prepared for my needs long ago when my parents gave me the funds for "a rainy day." If this emergency didn't fit that category, I didn't know what did.

I was amazed at how the situation changed when I looked for solutions instead of setbacks. Assets had been at my fingertips all along.

As you examine your own position, identify the obstacles that are preventing you from taking the risk to seek healthy change.

If you are isolated, what can you do to find allies? If you fear insufficient economic support, how can you earn or save more money? Can you take on an odd job, such as pet sitting or window washing? Do you have something valuable that you could sell to start an emergency fund? Could a bake sale or garage sale benefit you?

Fortifying Resolve

Make no mistake—choosing to enforce changes requires work, and lots of it. With the same dogged determination I'd used to sustain my marriage on artificial life support, I pursued a path to freedom. I talked with the investment broker to authorize the stock sale and visited the local bank's branch manager. The bank officer wrote a letter to real estate agents qualifying me as a purchaser based on my teaching job. Next, I asked friends for the name of a good agent and requested that person show me listings in my price range.

I felt proud of myself for accomplishing all that on my own. In less than four weeks, I had navigated the difficulties of contracting to buy a house as a single person, while maintaining a full-time job. Why had I wasted so many years feeling helpless and incapable of handling business arrangements? God guided me to what I needed, then he allowed me to choose when and how I would act.

God will do the same for you when you are ready to make changes. Be grateful as unexpected resources appear. Also, stay prayerful because your spouse may try to control you in other ways if financial blockades don't work.

Wendell sought to undermine my confidence with criticism by mocking my appearance. For example, one morning while I was showering, he opened the bathroom door and walked in without knocking. While I hurried to turn off the water and scrambled for a towel, he stared at my nakedness through the clear panel.

"One of your breasts is bigger than the other," he said. Then he chuckled and left room.

Over the years, I had discounted Wendell's emotional attacks since they weren't physical. But they entrapped me as surely as actual blows—maybe more so, because I questioned my sanity instead of connecting the dots to Wendell's erratic behavior and his domination over me.

His laughter about my body wounded me, and his critical eye made me feel shabby. Looking in the mirror, I let the towel slip and saw that Wendell was right. How had that physical defect escaped my notice all these years? A part of me that used to be attractive had become undesirable with just one comment from Wendell.

I noticed unsightly wrinkles and dimples on my nearly forty-year-old skin. A scar on my abdomen from an emergency appendectomy added to my imperfections. Had Wendell stopped loving me because aging made me ugly?

The face looking back from the mirror reflected sorrow. Who was I anyway? Surely a woman was more than her physical attributes. This body had birthed and nursed two fine sons and given love freely. So what if it revealed mileage from a full life? I had a good mind and a caring heart. These should matter more than my exterior.

God, do you love me? If I'm made in your image, does that make me beautiful?

I recalled a Bible passage describing the infinite care God uses to craft each person: "For you created my inmost being; you knit me together in my mother's womb" (Psalms 139:13).

Squaring my shoulders, I picked up the blow dryer and declared aloud, "If people think my breasts are ugly, they don't have to look at them." I set my focus on the future. But with each step I took forward, Wendell parried with attempts to block me, hoping I'd lose heart or fail, as I had many times before.

Domestic violence is defined as "a pattern of behavior in any relationship that is used to gain or maintain power and control over an intimate partner."[33] Mechanisms for control aren't limited to physical harm. Emotional and psychological intimidation also fit in this category. "You may be in an emotionally abusive relationship if your partner calls you names, insults you, or constantly criticizes you."[34] One woman recognized a subtle example of this negative behavior when she called home to talk with her elderly parents.

"I called and Dad answered. He and I had a great visit. Dad consoled me about losing my job, saying 'Making a home is valuable work.'"

"Then he asked me, 'Do you want to talk with your mom?'"

"Sure."

"I don't know where she is. Oh, here she comes—riding on her broom."

The woman told me, "Dad's derogatory reference to witches wasn't funny. His remark disrespected my mom, who had been sweeping the kitchen. Dad didn't realize how his snide comment about my mother undercut everything he'd just said to me about the value of being a housewife."

Do you also notice examples of disrespect in your relatives? The examples that were set for you as a child often will be repeated by you in adulthood. Acting differently requires learning new styles of communication.

Once you remove the blinders of helpless loyalty, you quickly see how your loved one tries to manipulate you. You are able to recognize control techniques, such as putdowns. Take satisfaction in knowing that when you shield yourself from mean comments, you are well on your way to beginning recovery. This journey to healing is a long one. Doubts will plague you, even as you progress. You'll wonder if you can manage on your own, but don't give up.

I had no guarantee of success, but what fueled my momentum was finally admitting to myself how miserable I'd been. I had nothing to lose. When Wendell realized that I had a closing date in a week, he began to backpedal. "C'mon, Lydia, you're not really going to leave, are you?" he asked, watching me put photo albums in a cardboard box in the basement.

I faced him squarely. "Yes, I am. You've pushed me too far this time."

"What can I do?"

"Could you please carry that heavy file cabinet out to the garage for me?"

Looking crestfallen, he wrestled the cabinet to the garage, then turned and went upstairs. I thought about all the dreams we'd planted together; these would be left behind like the flower gardens outside that I'd lovingly tended for years. Refocusing on the task at hand, I put knickknacks into another container and finished packing. When I came to the nicely framed portrait of me in my wedding dress, I threw it in the trash bin.

Torn Between Love and the Need to Protect Yourself

Emerging from codependency means separating yourself from your partner. Like the smaller Siamese twin, you fear that with parting from the larger person, you might cease to be. However, you must begin the emotional detachment if you want to survive as an individual.

Despite my mind's resolve to pursue change, my heart hurt. I didn't stop loving Wendell just because I no longer trusted him. You won't stop loving your spouse, either. When you've spent years with someone, the thought of leaving brings no real joy, but you still have to get relief from chaos. And you have a right to peace.

A day before the closing on my house, Wendell asked me to sit down in the living room and talk while the boys were at a neighbor's house visiting friends.

"Lydia, there's something I need to tell you, and I'm not sure how." He looked down at his right hand, where white knuckles gripped a notebook.

Part of me hoped he'd offer a genuine apology and extend an offer to meet me halfway. Could he be having a real change of heart? Curious, I leaned forward. "Go ahead."

"The other day, when I sat in the tree stand in the woods, God reminded me of something that happened when I was eight years old. Here's a school picture of me from then."

Wendell held up the marble composition book, which had a small photo taped on the cover. I saw a freckled boy smiling at the camera, his dark hair slicked back from a prominent cowlick. He wore an ironed plaid shirt, and innocence radiated from his trusting face.

"What happened when you were that age?"

"A close relative sexually abused me." Wendell's painful secret rushed out in a torrent of words. "It happened on and off a few years until I became strong enough to protect myself. I've never told anyone that before—not even my dad or mom."

Shocked, I tried to process this information. I understood personally the confusion a child experiences when wronged by an adult. My first French kiss came when I was eight years old, and the person who kissed me was my great-grandfather. Memories of his stale breath and wet tongue tormented me for years.

Grandpa had been a lonely widower who often spent summers with us. I cherished the times we read books together and worked in the family garden, cultivating sun-ripened tomatoes and prickly green okra. But his inappropriate act changed everything.

I had been taught that children should respect and obey their elders. Awkward and confused, I had had no idea how to respond to his violation.

Unlike Wendell, I had been able to confide in my mother, who listened and believed me. She told me I didn't have to accept that kind of attention. The next day, Mom explained to me that Grandpa had been told never to do that again.

But a few days later, when Mom and Dad weren't home, Grandpa tried to force another kiss. Armed by Mom's private counsel, I told Grandpa, "No!" and pushed him away with the puny strength I had. Grandpa never bothered me again.

Mom had broken the cycle of abuse by empowering me to say no. Her gift protected me as a child—and her validation factored into my being able to save myself as an adult.

Wendell's obvious distress convinced me of the sincerity of his confession. The relative who'd abused him had had many problems, including alcoholism, and a shady history the family rarely mentioned. Other relatives of Wendell had shared with me their concerns about that person, too. But I had no idea my husband also had been hurt.

Wendell sobbed. I held him as a mother would comfort a wounded child, all the while murmured assurances that he had done nothing wrong.

"That's when I took my first drink," Wendell said. "Booze helped make the pain go away."

This revelation placed missing pieces into a complicated puzzle. I now understood Wendell's false bravado and his inability to trust. My heart ached at the thought of him as a youngster being abused, afraid to tell anyone what happened.

"Maybe if I'd told someone sooner, things with us would be different," he said.

I wasn't sure how to respond. Was Wendell breaking down barriers to improve things between us? Or unloading a problem since he no longer thought my opinion of him mattered? I didn't want to be cynical, but Wendell had betrayed my trust too many times. I didn't want to let him use my empathy against me.

"I'm glad you shared this," I said. "It explains a lot about problems we've had over the years. Are you going to get help now?"

"I'm not sure."

"Wendell," I said, "this knowledge explains the past, but it doesn't change our future unless you're willing to do things differently."

Many times in the past, when Wendell had opened his heart, I'd collapsed into a puddle of compassion, letting the issue at hand become muddied and obscured. Although I cared about Wendell's suffering, I knew he needed to take responsibility for his behavior as an adult. I, too, had been harmed as a child, but I didn't want to let those bad experiences destroy a wholesome future.

If I didn't step up now and address formerly taboo topics, what might happen to Steve and Luke as they got older?

The disease of alcoholism affects the whole family, not just the individual with the problem. Often, the roots of addiction began in previous generations with abuse that occurred in childhood and went untreated. Psychologist and author Donald Dutton believes that many batterers have themselves been victimized and suffered trauma as children.[35]

Full recovery is not as simple as just not drinking or using drugs. In addition to biological complications, there can lurk serious emotional issues. True healing often requires a multipronged approach, including therapy for emotional wounds, medical care for physiological restoration, and reconnection with God for spiritual growth.

Clay, the gentleman in AA mentioned in chapter two, uses his own personal struggles and years of experience in recovery to mentor many people who want to heal from alcohol addiction. He advises family members who have someone suffering from alcoholism to carefully choose a neutral time for direct conversation about their concerns.

"I'd suggest you avoid using an accusatory tone. Use 'I' statements instead of casting blame with 'you' comments," Clay said. "Try something like, 'Honey, your drinking really scares me and this is how I feel when you drink.'"

Clay continued, "If your partner is not ready to do the work of recovery, you still have to protect yourself. Get involved in a support group that can help you learn how to handle the situation."

New knowledge is vital to combat addiction and its generational effects on families. For example, three of my four biological grandparents were alcoholics. Although my parents mitigated these circumstances as best they could in how they raised my siblings and me, certain unhealthy coping mechanisms were repeated.

It takes gumption to tackle the many-headed monster of addiction in a family. But you must remember that you have what it takes to overcome. You've already survived much danger, and you have the courage to keep climbing. Your family is counting on you to show them the way out.

Healing Practice #4: Expect to feel deep grief about your losses, but don't settle for quick fixes to stop the pain.

After the initial burst of anger-motivating change goes away, falling back into old habits can seem easier than continuing to face unknowns. Hold fast and let God secure you amid changes that take you to a better future.

Study Questions

1. What advantage do abusers receive when they keep others off balance by attacking or criticizing?

2. Think about compliments that people, other than your spouse, have paid you. What abilities do others see in you? What makes you unique? When was the last time you gave yourself credit for doing something well?

3. Identify places of refuge. Can you find moments of peace in a gym, on a nature walk, or sipping cappuccino at a coffee shop? Spend time in a location where you feel safe, even if it's a warm bathtub filled with bubbles. Use that quiet space to think about what you want.

4. What are ways your spouse shows he or she cares? How does he or she handle pain and confusion about problems?

5. Can your partner communicate ideas for specific ways to make the relationship healthier? Does your loved one demonstrate consistent effort to implement those improvements?

6. Do you have a family secret that haunts you and causes feelings of shame? Ask God to help you find healing so early traumas don't leave you stuck.

Resources

The Search for Freedom: Demolishing the Strongholds that Diminish Your Faith, Hope and Confidence in God is a book by Robert S. McGee that explores ways to overcome past wounds, such as insecurity and poor self-esteem. Vine Books, an imprint of Servant Publications, published the book in 1995.

Another excellent book for changing thought patterns is Joyce Meyer's *Battlefield of the Mind: Winning the Battle in Your Mind,* published by Harrison House in 1995.

Cecil Murphey wrote *When A Man You Love Was Abused.* This book guides women in helping their partners overcome childhood sexual molestation. Murphey's personal insights and sensitive approach offer suggestions for healing with a scriptural basis. Kregel Publications released the book in 2010.

STAGE TWO:

SWIMMING

You begin to establish a separate identity and withdraw from codependent behaviors.

C H A P T E R | F I V E

Upward Strokes

*O*nce you decide to leave behind the island of codependency, you have a chance to move toward a new horizon. You turn your back on the former identity as a helpless victim who is drowning and begin to see yourself as a resilient survivor swimming toward a better place. You want to improve your lifestyle and know you are capable of making changes.

But long-distance swimming requires strength and perseverance. You may get muscle cramps as you explore the vast, unknown waters stretching ahead.

"When things get too overwhelming, tuck them away," Vivian, a victim of domestic violence, advises about the early stages of healing. "I started drawing on my inner strength. As I got stronger, I learned how to deal with things, one at a time."

Keep putting one arm in front of the other, pulling forward in gentle strokes to reach an understanding of your wonderful traits and the amazing possibilities for your future. Leave behind the sad chapters of a haunted family history to embrace the good at your fingertips.

Though Wendell and I had suffered childhood wrongs, we had our health and two fine sons. I wasn't willing to jeopardize wonderful prospects because of bad things that occurred in the past. Wendell and I weren't children anymore to be terrorized by adults who had their own issues. The old hurts did not have to remain as excuses. Instead, the painful encounters could become reasons to improve our family dynamics.

Wendell and I had the power to choose how we wanted life to be in the future. I refused to excuse bad behavior because of old trauma. With no alteration in Wendell's outlook or behavior, I chose to keep going ahead alone. But I didn't get any applause for the effort.

I signed documents in the real estate office and began to redesign my life. I hoped Wendell and the boys wanted to grow with me, but I wasn't going to hold back, waiting to see if they would. I couldn't force them to change, but I could no longer remain stagnant.

On moving day, while the boys were at school, I said good-bye to Wendell as a friend's husband helped me load boxes and a few pieces of furniture into his truck. Mom and one of my siblings had flown in to help me set up the new household. While they organized the kitchen and bathrooms, my friend's husband helped me transport the dogs and doghouses to their new yard. Three close girlfriends brought housewarming gifts and flowers to my new place. But the occasion felt more like a funeral than a celebration.

While Mom and my sister helped arrange furniture, they questioned me about the boys' well-being. I didn't know how to respond. For weeks, I had tried to prepare them by looking at property and talking about moving; I didn't know what else to do to lessen their trauma. The only thing I knew for sure was that I couldn't live in the same house as Wendell and be safe. Although I had planned for the boys to be with me in the new place, my sons weren't ready to leave their dad.

The boys had a sports awards ceremony that evening, but I didn't think I had enough strength to attend after a night of no sleep and a full day of physical labor and emotions.

My mother and my sister got angry.

"You've got to go," Mom said. "The boys need to know you still care about them."

I argued my case, but she acted like I was a terrible person to even think of staying home. So Mom, my sister, and I went to the ceremony in chilly silence and sat in the auditorium. I saw Wendell sitting alone near the stage, and sorrow sprang up in my heart, but I locked down the emotion as soon as I felt it. I couldn't afford to be sentimental right now or I'd collapse.

Following the school program, Luke rode back to my house and Steve went home with Wendell. My mother and sister left early to stay in a hotel, saying they wanted to be closer to the airport for their next day's departure.

After Luke had gone to sleep in the other bedroom, I lay on my bed, listening to the quiet of the new place. I panicked at the monumental choice I'd made, and guilt and fear overwhelmed me. Was I doing the right thing? Could I make the mortgage payments? What if I failed? I spent the rest of the night throwing up in the bathroom.

If this sounds familiar, keep in mind that you might not know for sure that you've made the best choice for a long time. In the meantime, take consolation in the fact that drastic changes have to occur if you are going to survive. Dying little by little with each disappointment or wound is torture. At least when you leap into thoughtful action, you can brace yourself for impact.

In the morning, when the alarm went off, I awakened Luke. We got ready and hustled to the high school, where Luke was a sophomore and Steve, a senior. Getting through work that day took determination. I numbed my emotions to sustain the routine of what had to be done. I had set new goals and meant to see them through.

Sometimes, the only difference between success and failure is the sheer will power to keep going until progress is made. You have to grit your teeth and pour your entire body and soul into an endeavor because you know deep in your heart that what you are doing is right.

It doesn't matter how many people criticize you or don't understand your motivations. You have to fulfill a promise to yourself: you will give your all to achieve a worthy goal, or die trying. That's the difference between treading water and swimming—you move so far away from the familiar place where you used to make do that you have to keep going to find a new place to rest. There's no going back.

Implementing Change Includes Pain

When you take on the challenge of making changes, expect to feel pain. Sorrow and fear will accompany you on the journey, but they take on different shapes, and they soften and blur with time as you get through each day seeing what you can accomplish.

For me, life took on a surreal rhythm in which my body moved, but my mind and heart remained frozen. Each day, I concentrated on simple tasks, such as unpacking another box or raking the yard, to hold at bay the fear that I'd fail in this attempt at independence.

In their book *When Love Hurts*, co-authors Jill Cory and Karen McAndless-Davis describe the emotional yo-yo many experience between rebuilding and grieving.[36] While taking positive steps forward, those seeking healing also deal with sorrow over loss. Recognizing and handling frequent shifts from optimism to despair is part of the daily, and sometimes hourly, recovery process.

In my case, the greatest agony revolved around missing my sons. At the time, I didn't understand that their refusal to join me may have been motivated by the greater fear of losing their father. Cory and McAndless-Davis write that it is common for children to align themselves against a safe and dependable parent, precisely because they know they can act out difficult emotions without fear of reprisal. The authors also indicate that children often gravitate toward the adult they perceive as being the most powerful as a survival skill.[37]

All I knew was that I wanted my sons with me. Their absence caused a constant ache in my heart, and I hoped that if I kept leading the way, they would follow.

Steve stopped by three nights after the move to help me hang a few pictures that my mother had painted and given me over the years. While we measured where to put a nail, I said, "My mom and sister feel that I abandoned you and Luke. Do you feel that way?"

"No."

"There's room for you here. I'd love to have you stay with me."

"Yeah, Mom, I know. But all my stuff's at the other house, and that's where I spent my childhood. I want to be there."

Had I understood how much that house meant to the boys, I would have fought Wendell for who got the residence. Now it was too late.

I did the best I could to stay connected with my sons, often picking Luke up in the morning and taking him to school. Sometimes Wendell would invite me over for dinner with him and the boys. Those times eating meals together were bittersweet, but I appreciated getting to see the kids. Wendell acted happy to have me around, but he made no effort to address our marital problems.

My agony and loneliness were so great I thought I would explode into a million pieces. I knew I needed to get professional help to work through these huge issues; the burden felt too heavy for me alone. Fortunately, my job's insurance plan included mental health care.

Unwilling to suffer another disastrous encounter like the one with the counselor after my honeymoon, I asked my trusted friends for a therapist they'd recommend. One friend suggested I contact a lady named Reba, who had counseled for many years and had a solid reputation.

During our first appointment, Reba showed me warmth and caring. She listened attentively and asked questions to clarify my thinking. She didn't tell me what to do, but gave me an opportunity to assess my choices.

When I told her about Wendell complaining that I was rude to his family, Reba said, "The issue with the relatives wasn't a lack of hospitality. You broke the hidden rule in dysfunctional families by exposing alcohol."

My first session with Reba assured me that I was thinking clearly and the underlying issues about alcohol needed to be addressed. She helped me see a broader picture that made me realize I wasn't alone in my experiences. Being heard and believed unlocked places in my heart. I agreed to meet with her on a weekly basis.

A few days later, at work, an older teacher caught me in my classroom before the students arrived. "I know you're going through a hard time," she said. "I'm married to an alcoholic, and my twenty-six-year-old son just got arrested for driving under the influence. I wished I'd done a long time ago what you're doing now. Maybe my son's life would be different."

She patted my hand and turned to go, leaving me speechless. Never before had she confided in me on such a personal level. Her thoughtfulness humbled and encouraged me.

In your journey to wholeness, you also will find unexpected places of encouragement where you will realize that you are on the right path. God will place people in your life to ride alongside you and cheer you on. Like a support team navigating in a nearby boat, you'll have coaches to guide you across the rough channel. With them, you'll receive relief from the pain of doubt.

Envision Dreams to Keep Going

Even with support, you'll have to keep envisioning the dreams of what can be to carry you through the dark nights when endless waves of frustration wash over you.

Two weeks after the move, I awoke to a dull, cloudy Saturday morning. As I scanned the dingy backyard, I longed for the gardens I'd left behind. Rain outside my window dropped the tears I couldn't afford to shed without risking a complete breakdown. I had a choice: lose myself in regret, or get busy planting new dreams. I prayed God would work a miracle, but in the meantime, I had things to do.

Donning old jeans and a gray sweatshirt, I went into the garage to get flower bulbs I'd recently purchased. I grabbed the shovel, headed to the front yard, and started digging, with rain and mud splattering my shoes. Each thrust of the shovel lifting clods of clay proved I had strength and could make improvements. Earthworms wriggled in the newly exposed ground. Quietly, humbly, they contributed to the beautification project, and they worked with no limelight or fanfare. Would I be able to do the same?

Perspiration flowed, despite the chilly morning. I gently lifted the bulbs out of the sack. Some were rotten and collapsed into powder upon my touch, like dreams deferred too long. Other bulbs already sprouted tender white shoots, showing promise their time would come. These I tucked into beds of ebony potting soil, sprinkled with a blanket of bonemeal.

In a few holes, I found the U-shaped larvae of Japanese beetles. These gray worms morphed into armor-plated green thieves that devoured entire bushes. Fears ate at me, too.

Keep planting, I told myself. *Trust God to deliver the results*.

Only a few bulbs remained unplanted when I started thinking about moles, those little underground critters that dined on tubers like Thanksgiving turkeys. What if all this work ended in nothing? What if the bulbs got eaten, and I never saw a single bloom?

Just then, a divine picture sprang to mind. Row upon row of mature daffodils, with lemon-colored petals and smiling tangerine faces, beckoned me to believe in a brighter future. This image encouraged me to see what could be, and not dwell on the barren soil before my eyes.

Holding back grief required too much energy, and I allowed tears to flow onto the ground and become part of nature's cycle to water new life. The acceptance of loss freed me to see a clearer vision—one of dancing leaves and a rainbow of blooms nodding in approval of my hard work and tough choices.

In the bitter moments when you want to give up, what dream will keep you going? Without that strong sense of purpose, you will find sustaining the effort difficult. You have to have a dream big enough to overshadow the inconveniences of your immediate struggle so that you can keep going forward.

For example, a friend of mine named Emily wanted to be a performer. During her marital separation, she started taking guitar lessons. The first few weeks, she would show me the raw skin on her tender fingers from plucking the strings. Over time, she developed calluses to protect her hands and practiced with other musicians. Today, she and her band book regular shows in our community.

Consider writing down the personal goals you want to achieve. For example, when you are financially independent, what purchase will you make to reward yourself? Will you upgrade your vehicle, plant roses in the yard, or get a new look? Keep these written objectives nearby as a reminder of what you are working toward.

Another way to motivate yourself is to cut out magazine pictures of something you want to do or see and tape them near your bathroom mirror. Where will you live? What kind of clothes will you wear? What will be the expression on your loved ones' faces when they see all that you have accomplished?

Brace to Bear the Burdens

You'll need to brace yourself to bear the burden of change. Upsetting the family routine won't win you any compliments.

I had to assume all of the financial risk and inconvenience changing residences. Wendell maintained his posture as the one wronged, lobbying the boys—and everyone else—to believe that I'd abandoned them.

"Momma doesn't love us anymore," he'd say to the boys, within my hearing.

This psychological attack weighed heavily on me. I missed the boys and wished our family could be together again. But I also knew beyond a shadow of a doubt that Wendell only welcomed reunion if he maintained control and had his needs met, without regard to mine.

We maintained an awkward association as we tried to figure out what came next. Could there be any resolution to our differences?

Wendell and I spent a Saturday in mid-December watching Luke's basketball tournament at another school. Between games, Wendell and I talked about practical matters involving our separation.

"I'd like to list one of the boys as a dependent on my tax return," I said.

"No," he replied imperiously.

"Why not? Then we'd each have one deduction."

"You're being controlling. You should ask me instead of telling me."

I rolled my eyes. "Is it OK if I include one of the boys on my tax return?"

"I'll have to check with my attorney to see if that'd set a precedent."

In times past, I'd accepted this one-way decision-making to maintain peace. Having a safe place to retreat allowed me to confront Wendell's selfishness. So I went a step further.

"I paid for the attorney who drew up our legal separation papers. I also reimbursed the mediator we consulted about property settlement. And our family's gym membership and health insurance come from my salary. What have you given in this period of *mutual* separation?"

"I've been doing all the cooking and cleaning since you left."

"That's hardly a gift to me. Besides, you're the one who chose to keep the house."

A long pause ensued. During his silence, I thought about all the household items I'd left behind. In the move, I took a couple of chairs, a desk, two lamps given to me by my grandmother, two patio chairs, and my personal belongings, such as clothing and jewelry. Everything else remained because I wanted the original home left intact, as much as possible, for the boys.

"I've gotten my own car insurance," I added. "What have you contributed?"

"I gave you a garbage can for the new house. And three rolls of wire you needed to fence in the dogs."

How generous.

"I even got you a tool box," he said. "That broke my heart. By giving it to you, I empowered you to do things for yourself, which meant I wouldn't be able to."

Do you utilize your talents as tools to take care of yourself?

I pictured the yellow plastic tackle box containing an inexpensive hammer, two screwdrivers, nails, and duct tape. Wendell's gestures often held more show than substance. However, empowering me to do for myself was an important concept. Hadn't I always had the ability, but chose to live in the shadows, serving Wendell instead?

When Wendell said it broke his heart to give me tools, did he mean he grieved losing control over me? Or did he regret the lost opportunity for us to build together?

This period of separation had demonstrated that I could do a lot. I didn't need Wendell's permission or assistance to achieve success. Why had I lived so many years as though I did?

By choosing to relinquish my power over the years, I had crippled us both. My weakness facilitated Wendell's domineering behavior, and that combination stunted healthy emotional growth in both of us. Wendell's insecurity played into my fear of abandonment, and we failed to develop a partnership where our strengths blessed each other.

When you look at your toolbox of life, what do you see? Is the box full of equipment that you know how to use? Think about the skills you have. Do you use them to benefit yourself and others, or do you hide them in a box that never gets opened?

Beware Physical Intimacy that Ignores Emotional Wreckage

Developing proficiency with tools requires practice. As you become more skilled at overcoming financial barriers and recognizing emotional traps, you need to be prepared for how the desire for physical intimacy can sabotage your steps toward independence.

In a healthy marriage, sexuality is a God-given gift that brings joy to both partners. However, in marital separation, physical desire complicates matters. Your body won't always cooperate with your mind's rules about no contact. Learning to manage the temptations associated with this involves challenges.

For me, the first test occurred in the school parking lot waiting with Wendell for the kids after a game. Wendell turned to me in the privacy of the car and asked, "Would you like me to brush your hair?"

In the past, that tender act always made me feel loved. But now, Wendell's inquiry invited an uncomfortable intimacy. Did he think that brushing my hair would somehow win me over, make up for the way he dodged responsibility and treated me with disrespect?

"No, thanks. Wendell, we need to work on our real issues."

Too often I had settled for physical closeness as a substitute for the lasting resolution of conflict. Although Wendell's offer was enticing, the logical part of my brain suspected a distraction, and I chose not to fall for the ploy.

He moved away from me and retreated into a surly silence, which used to send me scrambling for his forgiveness. Now I held a firm stance so we wouldn't fall back into the old pattern of arguing, then making up with syrupy talk and physical intimacy, without resolving our problems.

Wendell's sullen withdrawal confirmed his shallow intent. I used to wait expectantly for dropped morsels of affection, savoring them for weeks. But I was hungry for real food now, and small pieces of candy wouldn't satisfy me; a few crumbs on the floor did not make a banquet.

It is common for abusers to use physical intimacy as a means to exert control, and it is important that you do not fall for this. Use all of your self-control to ensure that your passion and affection for your spouse do not outweigh common sense when troubles arise. You'll have to find ways to curb physical appetites that might distract you from dealing with problems in lasting ways.

Expect Cruel Backlashes from an Abuser

In a dysfunctional relationship, interactions often take familiar patterns. If the abuser cannot manipulate by exerting power, using charm, or exploiting sexuality, then he or she will go underground by attacking the things you value. This often happens in shocking ways.

On the mornings I picked up Luke to drive him to school, I went inside the old house, turned on the little light over the thirty-gallon aquarium, and fed the fish. For years, I'd had a kissing gourami named Fred. His pearly scales shimmered like jewels, and he had grown from the size of a quarter to as big as my palm. Fred swam to the surface each morning as I dropped colorful flakes of orange, green, and red food. His miniature companion, Nemo, hovered beside the algae-covered castle, blowing bubbles. Because I hadn't figured out how to relocate the large tank, the fish remained with Wendell. If I didn't feed the fish, no one did.

The day I went inside to help Luke move his computer to my

new place, I noticed that the spot on the bookshelf where the aquarium used to be stood empty.

Wendell sidled up to me. "We drew straws for who would tell you the fish died." Noticing my stunned look, he laughed.

An incredible grief rose inside me. Salty tears leaked out. I felt guilty for not saving those fish; I should have known they were at risk. I couldn't stand to look at Wendell's face and went upstairs to help Luke.

Luke and I loaded his computer into my car, then left. On the way to my house, I recalled the time I went out of state for several days to care for my ailing grandfather. When I returned, my dog Peanut was missing. When I asked Wendell where she was, he shrugged, saying, "I guess she took off when we lit the firecrackers in the backyard."

Loud noises always terrified the little Lab. Why hadn't Wendell placed her safely in the garage? I called the vet's office and local shelters for a week, but never did find Peanut.

Even more horrible than Wendell's callousness was my blind acceptance. To blunt the cruel reality, I rationalized that someone else must be giving Peanut a better home.

How could I have been so stupid?

Injury to pets often occurs in homes where an abuser lives. Abusers can vent frustrations on animals to show absolute control over the household. Other reasons that an abuser may harm a pet include: teaching family members submission, preventing the victim from leaving, or retaliating for acts of independence.[38]

If you are concerned about a pet's well-being, you can contact your local humane society or veterinarian for assistance.

Knowing my fish had died slowly, from neglect, horrified me. Yet why was I surprised? Hadn't that occurred to me over the years? Small indignities had turned into larger ones as I numbly watched the things I held dear disappear. I let go of girlfriends Wendell didn't like and phased out activities I enjoyed that he didn't support. Gradually, Wendell's control had become so complete I rarely questioned what he said.

At least the dogs were safe with me this time.

Then a horrible thought hit me. *You got your dogs out, but what about your kids?*

I glanced at Luke seated in the car next to me, feeling grateful he was willing to brave Wendell's displeasure to spend time with me. But how long could Steve and Luke survive in the toxic environment of the unquestioning obedience Wendell demanded in exchange for his love?

Would I be able to get Steve and Luke to places of security before irreparable damage occurred? I knew the boys had physical strength, but they were no match for Wendell's manipulation. Two teenagers couldn't live with their father's irrational behavior and not be affected. But could I convince them to leave?

As I emerged from the stupor of surviving in a day-to-day environment of craziness caused by a spouse with an active addiction, I began to process situations more clearly. I gained the objectivity to see inconsistencies. I stopped doubting myself so much and understood how the constant back-and-forth from sweetness to meanness had kept me off balance.

I prayed Steve and Luke would be able to see beyond Wendell's distorted perspective. Maybe I could model enough character that they would notice good differences and choose another path.

But the only way they would learn an alternative was if I proved successful in this venture. I renewed my commitment to see this experiment in independence through. I would do whatever it took to guide my family away from diseased desolation to a healthy place of respect and growth.

If the person you love has ever damaged or destroyed something precious to you, keep in mind that the implied threat is not subtle: "I can harm what you value, and I can do the same to you." Don't give in to this intimidation. You have a right to know that things important to you will be protected and kept safe. You should not have to worry whether your possessions will be intact when you return.

If you have this type of concern, please don't underestimate the severity of the problem. Avoid making excuses and ignoring your pain. Convert your fear into another reason to take action.

Even as small birds fiercely defend their nests against larger attackers, so too can you come up with a plan to protect what you hold dear.

Healing Practice #5:
Take time to process changes, stabilize, and rest.

Plants that have been uprooted need an opportunity to settle and grow new roots before they can thrive. People are no different; in seasons of upheaval you need time and space to adjust.

Study Questions

1. Think about the flower bulbs I decided to plant in my new yard. Some had rotted in the bag, but others persisted in determined growth, even in the dark without soil. Can you think of dreams you have deferred or given up? What small step could you take this week to plant hope?

2. Consider this Scripture from Deuteronomy 28:12: "The Lord will open the heavens, the storehouse of his bounty, to send rain on your land in season and to bless all the work of your hands." How has God blessed you, despite the sorrows you may feel at this time?

3. Which item in a toolbox best symbolizes you? Are you a nail, which, though small, has the strength to hold boards together? Or are you a measuring tape by which others can gauge progress and growth?

4. How does your sexuality affect your decision-making process? What beliefs about your appearance cripple you? Ask God to show you how to handle these concerns.

5. Do you maintain any exercise routine that keeps you fit and relieves stress? Consider how beneficial even a fifteen-minute walk can be in helping you take care of your body.

6. What activities bring you joy? Is it making a mess in the kitchen creating a new recipe? Taking pieces of fabric and fashioning them into a stunning outfit? Does riding a horse in the mountains bring you pleasure? Do you like getting your hands greasy working under the hood of your car? Don't wait! Take time to do something that makes you happy.

Resources

Creative imagery helps the mind work toward transforming imagination into reality. *The Artist's Way* is a book about traveling a spiritual path to higher creativity. Authored by Julia Cameron with Mark Bryan, the text suggests tools for recovering a sense of self and features self-paced exercises for practice (G.P. Putnam's Sons 1992).

YMCA offers fitness programs in many communities throughout the nation. In cases of financial difficulty, scholarships may be given. For more information about what's available in your area, contact the nonprofit's headquarters at 1-800-872-9622.

CHAPTER | SIX

GOING SOLO

*I*mproving your life doesn't happen overnight; it requires grueling effort. Sometimes, the trial will feel like more than you can bear, but don't give up too quickly. Soon, you'll start seeing tiny signs of growth.

For me, finding peaceful sleep in an empty house night after night represented a huge achievement. Although I got to see the boys on occasion, they still chose to live with Wendell. This meant I had to face my worst fear—being alone. The life lesson I'd avoided in college came back to haunt me. Without the flurry of activity in a household full of people, I had to focus on myself.

The agony of adjusting to living alone buffeted me like I was floating on a tiny raft far out to sea, with no land in sight. The shore behind me was invisible, but nothing definite showed yet on the horizon. Time passed in a semiconscious state, where my lips blistered in the sun's heat. A feverish thirst for being with Steve and Luke tortured me.

When not at work, I often stared out the bay window in the living room, hoping to see my sons show up for one of their visits. Watching the neighborhood children play football in the quiet cul-de-sac brought back memories of Steve and Luke in happier days when they would bring friends over, gobbling cookie dough faster than I could mix it.

Outside, the neighbor's yellow Lab, Chance, slobbered on his prized tennis ball, racing back and forth between children throwing passes. His trim body radiated joy; I envied him.

A few days later, his forlorn eyes stared at me from his front window. His family had gone away for a holiday trip. Chance didn't like being left behind, and his full-bodied bellowing echoed through the neighborhood like air brakes on a semi-trailer truck. Although other neighbors fed Chance, he was accustomed to the adoration of three children, a housewife, and a master. He didn't like spending Christmas alone.

"Hey, where is everybody?" I imagined him asking. "What about me?" I could relate.

His lonely protests barraged me the next afternoon as I tried to nap. A compassionate part of me wanted to applaud Chance's determination. I wished I could howl in pain without worrying about social proprieties.

"My family's all busted up too," I might bark. "Someone come hold me. Somebody lead me out of this cold, lonely place."

Instead of wanting to silence Chance, I felt like applauding him. *Keep up the good work. Let the world know you need companionship.*

Meanwhile, I suffered in socially acceptable silence.

Everyone handles suffering differently; some people plaster smiles on their faces, pretending all is well, while others openly cry, going through tissues at a record rate. Which category do you fall into? Ultimately, any expression of your hurt is fine, as long as you make sure to forge ahead. The rewards just around the corner will amaze you.

Reaching Out in New Social Circles

As you attempt to achieve new goals, you'll need to reach out and invite other people into your social circle. Part of the healing process involves expanding support networks.

This thought probably frightens you because you've heard too many criticisms over the years. But ignore those old tapes of condemnation. You are free to express who you are. You have much to offer and others will delight in getting to know you. As you escape from an unhealthy image of yourself that others have imposed, you'll be surprised to realize how special you are.

I know from experience that this is not easy. In addition to establishing a new physical home, I had to work to create a better emotional residence, one in which I developed more self-confidence. Because the identity and sense of belonging I had in the former neighborhood disappeared, I had to meet new people and connect with them. Part of me feared how others would react. Would they judge me? I felt very vulnerable.

One night, around dusk, while I was collapsed on the couch in my pajamas and feeling depressed, I heard unusual sounds. Stampeding feet and giggles rushed toward my front door. A group of young carolers serenaded, "We wish you a merry Christmas."

I cowered on the couch, hoping no one would look in the window to see me in pajamas. Soon, the merry troop marched to a nearby house. Not wanting to be the Grinch, I pulled on a housecoat, grabbed a handful of candy canes from the kitchen, and ran after the kids, feet shuffling in my fuzzy slippers.

The children sang, "Now, bring us some figgy pudding," to an elderly couple next door. When they got to the line "we won't go until we get some," the old gentleman looked at his wife in discomfort. They obviously had nothing to give.

I called from the back of the group, "Hey, will candy canes do?"

The old couple's slumped shoulders rose in relief when the seven-year-olds turned toward me. As little hands grabbed the peppermint candies, my old blue housecoat billowed on a breeze of good will.

I missed my boys like crazy, but God didn't want me to cower inside and miss out on his blessings. He sent divine little singers to remind me I wasn't alone or abandoned. I needed courage to escape the prison of hopelessness and emerge to see the good life my heavenly Father offered. Many simple pleasures existed to lessen grief, and I had things to offer others. God would bring the music if I chose to listen.

As you listen to the radio today, consider the things you can be grateful for. Look for opportunities to reach out to neighbors or reconnect with old friends. What do you have that you can share with someone else?

Recognize the Danger of Nostalgia

As you focus more on yourself and start developing new social contacts, your need for your partner lessens. You forget what the constant fear felt like, and this can lead to a new problem. You might tend to look back and become nostalgic about the past. You could romanticize the good times, conveniently forgetting the crises.

After a few weeks of freedom, I began to miss Wendell. I thought about his crazy sense of humor. I remembered a time when he and the boys hung green pants on a clothesline in the garage to play a joke on me after they had read a Dr. Seuss book. My attention focused on the good times we'd shared. Wistfulness enveloped me and my resolve weakened.

Thinking about an expensive wool coat Wendell had surprised me with one winter when we had little money, I yearned for him to wrap his arms around me and promise that we could work things out. Before I lost courage—or came to my senses—I grabbed the phone and called him.

"I need you to hold me."

"How do I find you?"

Five minutes later, the doorbell rang. Wendell stood outside, wearing a blue windbreaker matching his eyes, and he held a plate covered with tinfoil. I stood aside so he could enter. He handed me the hot plate, venting the aroma of lasagna and garlic, then stood in the hallway with his hands in his pockets. He waited for me to lead him to the living room, where I set the plate on the coffee table, then sat on the couch.

He kept standing, not sure where to sit. I patted the couch beside me. This was the first time he had been in my new home. He sat next to me and studied the room. How did he feel, knowing I'd made this home without his help?

"Thanks for coming over. I've spent the whole day in prayer, and I'm not sure what to do about us." Without warning, tears sprang into my eyes.

Wendell's rough hands pulled me close. Gentle strokes along my forehead calmed me. Was it only a few days ago I'd mocked his offer to brush my hair? Now his tender touch melted me, and his spicy cologne drifted into my awareness.

My head pounded from emotional exhaustion. What was the right thing to do? Words tumbled out as I tried to explain the feelings warring inside me. For an hour and a half, he held me, listening as his fingertips massaged my scalp and stroked my hair.

I reveled in his touch but thought my hair must look a mess. "This reminds me of the Bugs Bunny cartoon where the rabbit puts crazy things on Elmer Fudd's bald head." I giggled.

Wendell smiled. Our first date in college had been to visit his cousins, and we had watched Saturday morning cartoons with the children. Wendell had laughed louder at the characters' antics than any of the kids.

In the middle of revisiting this memory, part of me screamed, *What are you doing? This is the enemy!* But another part of me cuddled closer to Wendell's reassuring warmth and luxuriated in his undemanding caresses.

"Where do we go from here?" I asked.

"To the foot of the cross, holding hands all the way and staying on bended knees."

His spiritual response shocked me. Was God changing Wendell's heart?

Fatigue took over in the peaceful quiet, and I couldn't stifle my yawns. Wendell stood to leave. We embraced at the door, but I didn't want to let go.

I thought about throwing myself at Wendell and asking him to stay the night. Instead I said, "I don't want to be together out of need, and I'm really vulnerable right now."

He nodded.

"I want us to be together out of desire, when we're both strong and healthy."

He hugged me tighter, then dropped his arms and walked out the front door, broad shoulders hunched in his jacket. His cologne lingered on my collar as I yearned for what could not yet be. We had much work ahead to reconstruct ourselves and become whole again. I didn't want to take any shortcuts that gave me temporary relief from pain, but did nothing to solve our deeper problems.

After Wendell left, I put on flannel pajamas and crawled under the cold covers, wondering how I could get through another night alone.

When recalling fond memories of your loved one, treasure the recollections but don't let them derail you from your path to healing. Understand that each of you has good points and acknowledge those. Does your partner have a great sense of humor or dance well? Value those positive attributes without letting nostalgia trip you up from addressing important issues like safety and respect.

Seek Wise Counsel

Trying to navigate your way around all of these complications gets confusing, and you need wise counselors to help you untangle all the mixed-up concerns. You want your family reunited, but how can you be sure that anything will improve if you go back now?

The temptation to quit my heroic pursuit of change grew strong as the effort to reinvent myself and relationships with the people I loved proved harder than I'd thought. I had underestimated their resistance and felt a strong riptide from their united front try to tow me back to the ways things had been.

Sometimes I wondered if all the pain I was experiencing was worth the effort. I alternated between holding my course and running back to Wendell, particularly as he kept the boys as his trump card.

I thought my head might burst if I kept all the what-ifs locked inside, so I needed to get feedback from trusted advisors. I knew they couldn't give me the answer, but at least being able to share concerns would help me organize the thoughts running around pell-mell in my mind.

I called my friend Brian, a retired pastor, whom I'd known for years and had served with on a community prayer team. I could confide in him and ask for guidance about Wendell's religious talk.

When Brian answered the phone, I briefly explained the recent events. "If God is working with Wendell, I don't want to miss an opportunity to heal our marriage."

"You need to give him time to find his own relationship with God, not just to please you," Brian said. "He has to demonstrate that he's truly changed. Each of you needs individual healing to create a stronger foundation for any future relationship."

After thanking him for the advice, and praying with him, I left to meet Reba at my weekly counseling session.

"Lydia, you have wisdom," she said. "I think you're right to wait and test Wendell's level of commitment."

"How will I know if he's really changing?"

"He'll wait for you to rebuild trust in him, no matter how long that takes. He'll also acknowledge how he's hurt you and take responsibility for changing his behavior."

Reba gave me a safe place to share where I began to rediscover my inner self apart from Wendell. Her belief in my strength and capability gave me hope that I could craft a better life.

"What areas do I need to target to help myself?"

"Let's focus on setting clear boundaries for what you want from others. Think also about how you can be more specific in expressing your expectations."

She smiled. "Be sure to take care of yourself too. You've got lots going on right now."

After I left Reba's office, I called my attorney, Hattie, to cancel a meeting. Questions of property settlement, custody, and tax filing exhausted me. I decided to take time to read the Bible:

"I removed the burden from their shoulders; their hands were set free from the basket [Egyptian slavery]. In your distress you called and I rescued you" (Psalms 81:6–7).

Despite yearning to know what the future held, I trusted God had a plan for good. My body couldn't carry the heavy burden of what-ifs, so I offered up my concerns in prayer.

Dear Lord, I need your help holding the weight of uncertainty. Please keep Steve and Luke safe. Please help me do a good job at work and trust you to bring healing. Amen.

Having conversations with my pastor-friend and therapist helped me sort through what I was feeling. These confidantes had no personal interest or bias to direct me to a particular action. Instead, they gave me an emotional refuge where I could analyze my choices.

Confiding in stable, insightful people protected me from making rash decisions. Remember to consult people you trust to help sort out your feelings. Seek out more than one advisor to share ideas with and consider many possible solutions. Try to stay away from emotionally involved parties, such as relatives or friends, when you are analyzing what is the next best step for you.

Set a Sustainable Pace

Chasing your goal of a better life is hard work. You are in this for the long haul and need to rest every now and again. Otherwise, you'll burn out and not be able to sustain the steady pace required to achieve your dreams.

Looking back, I realize that weeks passed before I was able to develop some semblance of a normal routine. I still ate dinner on occasion with Wendell and the boys at our old home, but felt like a visitor. Little pictures and knickknacks that made the house feel like home had been replaced by others that had nothing to do with me.

I sometimes called Steve and Luke to do things with me, but they usually said they were busy or tired. I understood their anger but didn't know how to reconnect with them. Maybe my sons locked me out to protect themselves from false hopes; they also suffered from the marital chaos. How could I explain that a temporary bandage of just moving back in with them wouldn't fix anything in the long run?

If I gave up now, all the hardship would be wasted and nothing good gained. Wendell would get back a flimsy cardboard wife, and I would lose any chance to find myself. The boys would learn women could be manipulated and had no strength. Was that the legacy I wanted to leave my sons?

Running late after tutoring a student one day, I hurried to make the scheduled appointment with a marriage counselor Wendell had hired for us. I wanted to make the first session on time.

A yellow school bus lumbered on the road in front of me, put on flashing lights, and stopped. Traffic halted while a small girl wearing a dress and tights bounced down the bus steps, then skipped to her house near the road.

The seven- or eight-year-old child grabbed the knob of the front door and turned, but nothing happened. She paused a moment, then knocked. Meanwhile, the bus driver waited, and the line of traffic grew.

Dropping her book bag, the girl used both fists to beat on the door. The bus driver called out something, to which the girl shrugged. Then she kicked the door.

I wanted to kick too as precious minutes ticked by. Traffic waited as the driver yelled again, and the child returned to the bus. She jumped on, and the yellow haven rolled away. Gratitude toward a bus driver, who cared enough to wait and offer refuge to a little girl, overcame my frustration about the delay.

Like that child, I kept finding locked doors. I went to familiar places but didn't have the key for entry.

Our new therapist, like that bus driver, gave me a safe place to rest. She listened to my concerns about the marriage. Although she didn't have magic answers, she offered hope by pointing out that Wendell showed initiative by arranging for counseling.

Twenty years of dysfunction wouldn't get healed in a few weeks. I needed to settle as a passenger on God's bus and let him drive. With him steering, I could relax and take in the scenery.

When you feel exhausted, take some time to sit back and breathe deeply. Trust that God has you on a journey and that he will take you to a place of security and health.

Acknowledge Personal Flaws

While you let God drive the bus and you take a break, you might notice things about yourself that aren't quite right. Maybe you're impatient or jump to negative conclusions. Without your attention consumed by others, you can focus on areas inside you that need improvement.

I noticed flaws in myself when Luke and I embarked on a project at my new house to redecorate the den. We started by painting the walls a blue we both liked. We didn't finish before he had to leave, so Luke left his computer on a flimsy TV tray, surrounded by a sea of drop cloths and disconnected cords.

I waited a couple of weeks for Luke's return. When he didn't call or stop by, I took matters into my own hands and finished the room. A neighbor's son hooked up the computer for me.

Seeing the tidy new office gave me a sense of satisfaction. This accomplishment showed I could establish order from chaos, which boosted my confidence. I wanted to share activities with the boys, but it was important that I not be dependent on them, or anyone else.

The next time Luke visited, he made a beeline toward the den and came to a standstill when he saw the completed room, with a desk holding his computer. Anticipating praise, I smiled.

But he reacted with anger. "Why didn't you wait for me? I'm the only one who spent that first night here with you, and now you squeeze me out of the one room I thought was mine."

His attitude put me on the defensive. "I didn't know when you were coming back and I got tired of looking at the mess. Aren't you excited to see everything fixed up?"

Without answering, Luke lunged into the den and started shoving furniture. His temper scared me. For a moment, the sight of man-sized arms angrily slinging stuff around hid the child I loved. Panic filled me.

Should I allow Luke to take over and change the room so he'd be happy and stay? Or should I stand up for myself and require respect? This dilemma paralleled the problem I'd faced for twenty years with Wendell, and I knew caving in would accomplish nothing.

"Stop moving furniture," I demanded.

He paused, looking at me with hurt in his eyes.

My tone softened. "Let's talk."

"Take me to Dad's." He stormed to the garage and got into the car, slamming the door.

I followed in disbelief. The abrupt cut-off resembled Wendell's pattern. If I didn't do exactly as he desired, I got left behind. Ignoring problems only made them worse. How could I show Luke a better way to handle conflict?

With sorrow, I got the keys and sat in the driver's seat. I tried again to get Luke to talk. "Can you please explain what you're feeling?"

He looked sideways at me, but remained silent. In frustration, I started the car and drove to Wendell's house.

In the driveway, Luke turned to me. "Why didn't you call me to come help? Why do you keep secrets? Why do you have to control everything?"

Although his words hurt, I realized the honesty behind them. My take-charge approach left no room for partnership. Too focused on protecting myself, I'd trampled something he valued.

"I'm sorry about not waiting. I wanted everything to look nice and thought you'd lost interest. I didn't mean to be secretive."

He stared into my eyes as though trying to verify that I felt bad.

"This separation is difficult for all of us," I added. "Relationships shouldn't be based on win-lose, with one person always getting his way and the other losing every time. At some point, you're probably going to marry a stubborn and strong-willed woman. You need to learn how to communicate without somebody always having to lose."

He stared at the dashboard. "We figured if we boycotted you long enough, you'd come home begging."

Luke's blunt statement stunned me. Did Wendell encourage the boys to leverage their affection so I'd yield?

"That's a sad relationship, don't you think?" I said softly.

He kept his head down.

With Wendell, marriage had been a contest of wills. Steve and Luke witnessed this constant tug-of-war, and I didn't want them to think that was the way men should treat the women they loved.

As we continued talking in the car, Luke and I made progress toward understanding each other, though we didn't completely resolve all the issues. Finally, he got tired of talking and left me in the car, without any commitment for when we would get together again.

I drove home, sad that my opportunity to be with Luke had disappeared. As much as I wanted someone else to be the culprit, I had to own part of the problem. I should have called Luke and asked for a specific time when we could finish the project. If he wasn't willing to commit to that, at least he would have had the chance to be included.

I mistakenly assumed his absence meant rejection. Maybe he had simply been busy. How often had my insecurities led to reactions that damaged the boys? I needed to learn how to speak up and find compromises.

God, help me not to crawl back into a hole of dependence because I'm too weak. Please give me wisdom so I can face this terrifying aloneness and figure out how to break the cycle of domination and dependence.

Silence in my empty house suffocated me, while barren rooms mocked me. Did God hear my prayers? Then a thought popped in my head: Christ himself prayed for me.

Christ Jesus, who died—more than that, who was raised to life—is at the right hand of God and is also interceding for us. (Romans 8:34)

Despite my guilt and shame over a ruptured marriage and failing as a mother, Jesus still loved me enough to speak to the

Father on my behalf. Jesus had healed the blind, mute, diseased, bleeding, paralyzed, and possessed; surely his touch could restore me. Trusting in his unconditional love involved risk, but it was the only medicine I knew for healing a broken heart.

When you take a hard look at yourself, can you be honest about weaknesses you see? Can you admit areas that need God's healing touch, without blaming anyone else for your short-comings? Take time to acknowledge areas where you fall short and ask God to help you heal these so what you offer your loved ones is the best possible you.

Healing Practice #6: Relationships of respect do not require one person to sacrifice dearly held values.

If you have to give up everything you think is important to keep another person close, you are setting yourself up for heartache and failure. A partnership involves both people sharing and compromising.

Study Questions

1. What values do you hold dear? Write a list of things such as honesty, punctuality, etc. Do you enforce respect for these in your relationships? Or do you allow your values to be trampled so a relationship can continue?

2. Think about happy family memories you have. What made those times special?

3. When the carolers serenaded my house, I had a choice: enjoy the music and join in, or hunker down inside and tune them out. What opportunities do you have to hear joyous music, even if it's only on the radio or from a bird chirping? Are you ready to sing along? Carefree participation frees you to find happiness in the moment.

4. Are you tempted to take shortcuts to settle issues in your marriage? How can you protect yourself from throwing away the hard-won independence you've achieved so far?

5. Have you experienced an emotional boycott when some-one you loved cut you off from conversation? Withdrawal of affection is a powerful weapon of control. How can you prepare yourself to handle these tactics so you don't cave in to unfair demands?

6. How do children mimic relational patterns they observe in their parents? What can be done to educate them about healthy ways to relate?

7. What heavy burden are you carrying that you can release to God? Take quiet time to reflect. Read the Psalms in the Bible and underline passages that comfort you.

8. Prayer is a powerful weapon against discouragement and despair. Talking with the Lord doesn't have to be fancy or formal. Whisper to him today what's in your heart. He will hear, and if you quiet your heart to listen, you will hear him respond with loving words.

9. What's one area in which you'd like to improve? Do you need to learn how to balance a checkbook or put more effort into your personal appearance? Set a goal and get to work.

Resources

Encouraging lyrics can be found in the song "Walk with You" by Della Reese and the Verity All-Stars on the CD *Touched By An Angel* (1998). Another title on the album is "Believe in You" by Amanda Marshall, which rallies silenced voices to start singing their own tune again.

Melody Beattie's *Codependents' Guide to the Twelve Steps* (Fireside 1992) applies the principles of healing used in Alcoholics Anonymous to people recovering from addictive relationships. Her text also contains a resource guide for recovery programs.

To understand specific tactics that abusers use, refer to the next pages. There you will see the Power and Control Wheel and the Equality Wheel from the Duluth, Minnesota models. The diagrams, created by battered women in focus groups con- versations over several years, resemble spokes of a wheel and identify categories of manipulation, as well as healthier inter- actions. For more information, contact the Domestic Abuse Intervention Programs by calling 218-722-2781 or visit http://www. theduluthmodel.org/pdf/PhyVio.pdf.

Power and Control Wheel

Physical and sexual violence may occur sporadically, with years between violent episodes. Even one physical attack can be enough to terrify and contain a victim for a long period. Trapped by the constant threat of physical and sexual harm, a victim may experience other forms of an abuser's control as shown below.

DOMESTIC ABUSE INTERVENTION PROJECT

202 East Superior Street
Duluth, Minnesota 55802
218-722-2781
www.duluth-model.org

Equality Wheel

Participants in the Domestic Abuse Intervention Project also developed a graphic to illustrate healthy relationships. The Equality Wheel highlights patterns of shared responsibility and respect. Rather than fear, interactions revolve around fairness and nonviolence.

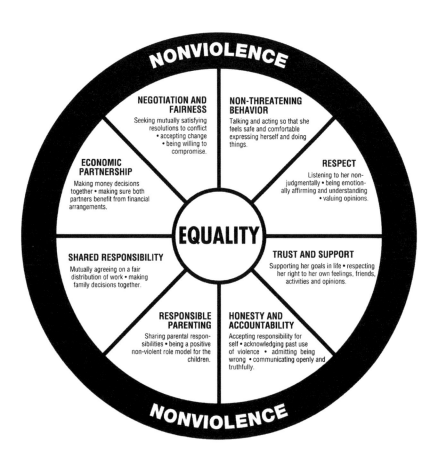

DOMESTIC ABUSE INTERVENTION PROJECT
202 East Superior Street
Duluth, Minnesota 55802
218-722-2781
www.duluth-model.org

CHAPTER SEVEN

Take Inventory for Personal Growth

*W*hen you ask God to heal your weaknesses, he will. Don't be surprised as he gives you awareness of the fact that you are well equipped to handle your situation. He'll give you an itemized list of ways in which you can grow and provide opportunities to practice. Yield to his gentle tutoring and you'll develop a new understanding of yourself.

As I reflected about the argument with Luke, I realized that I needed to evaluate how my emotions affected my interactions. Although I wanted to blame Wendell for all our problems, the truth was that I also contributed to breakdowns. I didn't know how to have healthy conflict. I thought disagreement meant one person yelled and won, while the other gave in, but held a grudge.

An opportunity to address this misconception occurred at church one weekend when the pastor used bananas in an illustration about whether or not we walked with the Holy Spirit. The lesson centered on showing the godly fruit of love, joy, peace, patience, kindness, goodness, faithfulness, gentleness, and self-control (Galatians 5:22).

To demonstrate, the minister invited a teenager to the stage, offering the young man a yellow banana to eat. The boy tasted the ripe fruit and smiled. Then the pastor held up an aged black banana. The congregation groaned in sympathy. The volunteer winced as soggy mush hit his tongue.

For me, the bananas represented two types of anger. The ripe fruit meant healthy, conflict-solving disagreements conducted in a timely and fair fashion. The rotten fruit stood for unaddressed problems, which caused simmering, silent resentments. Had I talked openly with Luke about feeling abandoned before finishing the den myself, a lot of heartache could have been avoided.

Years of feeling silenced and ignored left me feeding on the rotten fruit of hidden anger. Negative emotion became my anesthesia. As long as I focused on what other people did or didn't do, I didn't have to probe inside me.

Unresolved internal conflict can rob you of finding happiness. This is how one woman described rotten anger's effect: "Our neighbors split up because of alcoholism and domestic violence. We loved them both dearly. The man forgave, moved on, and eventually remarried, but the former wife is just as angry as she was eight years ago. Her rage is what sustains her. If she ever let go of that anger, she'd be a popped balloon with nothing left."

How sad to let trauma freeze you in a place of unrelenting upset. As long as a sour outlook dominates, there is no room for healing. Acknowledge hurts, but don't stop there.

Isolation provided me with time for reflection. Ninety days into the process of self-discovery, I saw my warts. Anger at others no longer shielded me from looking at my ugly parts. Controlling others had consumed me to the point where I'd lost my individual identity. Along the way, I also lost track of joy and peace by cramming my schedule full of everything except God.

I had let others choose who I was, or wasn't, and evaded

responsibility for defining myself because it was easier to let parents, teachers, or my husband tell me about myself. As long as I performed well, I thought people would love me. I had no clue God's love came without conditions. He didn't want me to *do* as much as he wanted me to *be* with him.

Believing self-worth came from actions ruined any chance of contentment because I could never do enough—not for Wendell or anyone else. That false concept of value based on effort set me up for an impossible situation, which only an increasing awareness of God's tenderness could counter. God wanted to teach me I didn't have to earn his affection.

I needed to stop savoring self-pity. With God's encouragement, I could leave behind thoughts about my inadequacy and stop whining about what other people failed to do. I committed to practice speaking up and braving direct conversation.

As you examine how you handle conflict, think about whether you hide your true feelings or turn into a raging lunatic. How can you modify your behavior to use reason instead of fighting? Do you cling to rage because you're afraid that if you let it go, you'll be empty inside?

Accept Reality

No matter how hard you try, sometimes you can't convince other people to change. You have to let them make different choices than you would. You accept that their reality is not what you want for yourself.

The weekend before Valentine's Day, I flew to Texas for my brother's wedding. Neither Wendell nor the boys wanted to go, and I felt anxious about the trip. Attending a family event alone highlighted my predicament. Also, my siblings and I had barely spoken since November. I didn't want to go to a wedding in the middle of my separation, but loyalty to my brother outweighed personal discomfort, so I prayed somehow I'd be joyful.

In church, watching the exchange of vows brought back many difficult memories. I still wanted to believe a miracle could happen for Wendell and me.

During the flight back after my brother's wedding, I considered my competing emotions. As I stared out the small plane window, I fiddled with the wedding band on my left hand. It circled round and round, much like our relationship, which never seemed to stabilize.

Twenty years, a vow to God, and two great kids hung in the balance. Not ready to quit, I decided to deliver Valentine's Day presents to Wendell and the boys on my return from the airport. But when I showed up, no smile greeted me at their front door—all three gave me a frosty reception. As no one had a gift or card for me, I slunk out of the house, feeling let down.

Steve followed me outside to my car. "Mom, people are calling here at all hours."

I wasn't sure what he meant. "Do you mean lots of women are calling your dad?"

He looked down, scraping the toe of his shoe on the driveway.

How my son must love me to disclose this. He felt honor-bound to protect me by telling the truth, but in doing so, he revealed private information about Wendell. I didn't want to embarrass Steve by asking questions.

"Thanks for telling me. I needed to know." I hugged Steve, then got in my car and left.

Keeping Steve's warning private, I chose not to confront Wendell because I didn't want to endanger Steve. Besides, what right did I have to ask for faithfulness? Hadn't I been the one to move out?

At home that night, I read a reassuring excerpt from Dr. Harriet Lerner's book *The Dance of Anger: A Woman's Guide to Changing the Patterns of Intimate Relationships*. Dr. Lerner wrote that women who are depressed and guilty lose any power to effect positive change. However, she also said that angry women have the potential to become agents for improved circumstances, both personal and social.[39]

My desire for a better life burned, not like a match soon to go out, but with the steady heat of white-hot coals under huge oak logs stoked with years of betrayal. This latest evidence of

Wendell's inability to be faithful should not have come as a surprise, but it still hurt.

I needed to accept the reality that life with Wendell always would involve uncertainty. It was time to quit living with the illusion he would change. Such a sad realization caused a great deal of pain. For far too long, my hard-held optimism had resisted the notion to completely give up on Wendell. The tendency to believe the best had kept me going for years.

Yet I knew I had to release Wendell and any expectations we could ever be husband and wife again. I knew what I needed, and I knew that he couldn't give it to me. That didn't make him wrong or evil, but it did free me from clinging to an arrangement that degraded me.

As you journey toward healing, you'll come to a point where you can't make any more compromises. You'll know for certain the limit to what you can give and tolerate. You'll know that you've done all that you can. And you'll find peace in that knowledge.

Release Others to Their Choices

Once you have accepted that there is nothing else you can do, your next step is releasing others to make their choices without blame or bitterness. Your job is to keep working on you and achieving the goals you've set for yourself.

After Steve's warning, I withdrew from contact with Wendell to focus on things I could do for my healing. Wendell sensed my distance and tried to woo me again. As we neared the four-month mark of separation, he called regularly, asking me to dinner at nice places. Although wary, I accepted his invitations because remaining silent did nothing to address our issues.

At one restaurant, he stared at me with longing and said, "You're beautiful." He added assurances of his steadfastness, saying, "I love you so much. If you were in a coma, I'd come read by your bedside on the chance you could hear me."

His comments felt like lines from a soap opera. I emotionally distanced myself from his dramatic show, reminding myself he hadn't bothered to come to the emergency room for Luke or me. Why did I think he'd look after me if I were comatose?

Wendell also acted vulnerable at the marriage counselor's office, and his voice held just the right note of earnestness. I got confused trying to figure out what to believe. Although I forgave the past, I didn't want an insecure future. Staying with Wendell meant always being on edge; I never knew what problem would hit or when. He never acknowledged how his inappropriate behavior hurt me or others.

Wendell knew my weak spot centered on Steve and Luke. In a show of including me in a parenting activity, Wendell invited me to go with him to take Steve for oral surgery to remove four impacted wisdom teeth. The next day, I stopped by Wendell's house after work to check on Steve, who could barely focus his eyes due to pain medicine. Steve had ice packs on his cheeks, and a slim line of blood edged his lip. I helped where I could, then returned to my place as evening fell.

Wendell called later. "When are you coming back home to us?"

I said, "You're in love with an image that's not me. I don't think you're going to be comfortable with the person I'm becoming."

A daring part of my mind made an odd proposal: *Tell him he needs to move on. See if he loves you enough to allow you freedom*. What did I have to lose?

I took a big breath and said, "You need to let me go. I can't go back in the little box where I used to live, trying to be what other people want me to be."

"Then I wish you well." His generous response surprised me.

I exhaled with relief. "I hope we can still be friendly. I want to see the boys and be with them. Is it OK if I stop by tomorrow to check on Steve while you and Luke are at the tournament?" Wendell planned to travel two hours the next morning for a regional match, and I worried Steve still needed care.

"No. It's not OK if you come to the house."

"Then why don't you bring Steve here in the morning on your way out?"

"The boys don't want to be around you."

"Wendell, don't use them as a power play."

"Steve can call you tomorrow, if he wants to."

"Steve can't hold his head up long enough to look at me," I said. "How is he going to be able to let me know if he needs something?"

"You have your pride and freedom, but that's all." The phone went dead.

I stared at the receiver. Wendell's true colors surfaced under pressure, and no grace remained. He compromised our sons to punish me, and I felt sad about his selfish cruelty.

The next morning I called Steve to see how he felt after the dental surgery.

"I'm OK," he mumbled.

"Do you want me to pick you up and bring you here so you won't be alone?"

"No, I'm fine."

"Would you like some soft food to eat?"

"That'd be great."

I gathered a care package of pudding, bananas, and pound cake, then drove to Wendell's house. I rang the doorbell and waited. Steve opened the door, then leaned against the doorframe while I handed him the bag of goodies. Puffiness and bruises dotted his cheeks, but at least he was mobile.

"Thanks," he said in a muffled voice, then closed the door.

I didn't know what to do. If I stayed with Steve or took him to my house, Wendell might make an ugly scene later. Torn between a desire to respect Wendell's privacy and a longing to care for my son's needs, I felt helpless.

During the two-mile drive back to my place, I reasoned that Steve could call me if he needed anything. The rest of the day I stuck close to the phone.

Feeling helpless is often part of the abusive cycle. Manipulators stack the deck so that no matter what choice you make, you can't win. However, the long-term victory comes when you stick to your standards and act with consistent integrity and honesty.

On Sunday I called to ask Luke about his tournament. We talked a moment, then somehow got embroiled in an argument about whether or not I'd betrayed his trust by sharing something he had confided in me with his dad.

"How can we resolve this conflict?" I asked.

The line went dead.

I picked up Melody Beattie's *Codependents' Guide to the Twelve Steps* and flipped to the page where I'd left off. She wrote that we need to remove ourselves as victims and learn how to find our own path.[40] Her insights encouraged me to keep walking forward and find the lovable aspects of myself that I want others to recognize and honor.

Melody's book also assured me that I wasn't alone in facing family problems surrounding alcoholism. I decided to find a group in my area that might help me learn more about the disease and appropriate coping skills.

I didn't like Wendell's choices, or Steve's, or Luke's, but I released them to make their own decisions. Slowly, I learned to let go of circumstances I couldn't control.

Control is an issue that you may find yourself struggling with. You want things to turn out right, so you make yourself crazy trying to influence everyone to your way of thinking. You can only do so much; then you have to let others assume responsibility for their acts. Love them where they are but allow them to find their own way.

Find Fellowship in Support Groups

Releasing loved ones so they can make their own choices may leave you lonely. To offset this feeling, you can attend support groups for codependents who want to develop individual strength and healthier relationships. You'll be amazed at the camaraderie that develops in a short period. Much like war veterans discussing maneuvers, you'll have a common language with other survivors of situations involving alcoholism and personal recovery from dysfunctional patterns. Group members will understand your raw pain because they've felt despair too.

One lady in the group I visited said, "I've been working my

program of recovery really hard, but I don't feel like anything's changing."

I knew what she meant. Weary and frightened, I wondered how to sustain the effort rebuilding required. One thing was certain: I couldn't go back. Wendell's continued deceit and cruelty killed any chance of us getting back together. I had exhausted every option for reconciliation. But could I keep moving forward?

Only God could give me an understanding of who I was becoming. After spending years denying my desires and whining about unmet needs, inviting God to take care of me revolutionized my outlook. His abundant gifts would come faithfully, right on time, without me obsessing or struggling. From that terrifying place of loss and aloneness, God brought hope.

Blessings came in many forms. Wendell offered me a single cash payment to relinquish my ownership in the old residence. That payoff gave me the money to reimburse the boys' college funds, as well as establish an emergency account. With this, many financial pressures subsided.

God also sent many people to shore me up during this time of reconstruction, and a circle of love surrounded me with sturdy threads of acceptance. Members of the support group assured me that I had value as a person. Despite the sorrow we shared in the meeting rooms, we also had laughter. I began to look forward each week to the sessions to see how others had met their challenges.

Please take time to find a support group that fits you. In this setting, you'll discover much about yourself from hearing others' stories. You'll find hope and strategies for overcoming problems. These groups provide literature that gives you a new understanding about dynamics that have affected you for a long time. You don't have to be alone.

Recovery isn't defined by how many support group meetings you attend or if you can recite from memory an organization's guiding principles. The true tests for healing are whether you feel a deep inner peace and are able to sustain healthy relationships.

Be wary of groups that try to impose their will on you. Healthy support networks offer options and affirm you as an individual. You don't want to trade one form of control for another.

Take Time to Play

As you discover new fellowship, you'll also begin to see more good things about yourself. You'll flourish in secure settings. Your confidence will grow, and you'll feel more capable of trying new things.

I dared to enroll in an art class. Something about bright, cheery colors welcomed me and promised to banish the darkness of many disappointments. Hoping to capture the exquisite design of a rose in bloom, I took watercolor painting lessons, something I'd always wanted to do. My initial attempts resulted in a splotch of muddied colors. Ruth, the instructor, saw my frustration.

"Let's try this." She loaded the tip of the paintbrush with paint, then flicked her wrist so drops of color spattered everywhere.

I laughed. In the midst of grief and attempting perfection, I had forgotten to have fun. Was art as simple as making a mess? I could do that!

With enthusiasm, I copied Ruth and showered dobs of wet paint on the canvas. But my abandon didn't have the same results as hers. Again, Ruth rescued me. She grabbed a bottle of sea salts. When she sprinkled granules onto the wet paint, the white paper came alive with pleasing geometric patterns of pigment.

"Try another color," Ruth said.

I mixed orange and red together, imagining the collision of hues. Instead, they combined into a delicate shade of peach.

Could I also allow clashing emotions to mix into a beautiful pattern? Processing sorrow made room for the joy of experiencing new things. The art class reminded me to see possibilities through different combinations.

"Take this hair dryer and chase the wet paint around," Ruth said, demonstrating how heat graduated shades of color.

Within an hour, I left with my first watercolor masterpiece. Ruth's gentle coaching encouraged me to enjoy the process, waiting to see what each experiment might reveal.

Maybe life was a watercolor painting in which God layered over mistakes to add depth and richness. He sprinkled the salt of adversity to define my outlook, and he used the heat of difficulty to dry up misconceptions and solidify values.

Though I faced a new battle since Wendell had filed in court for sole custody, peace rested in my heart. As more expensive litigation loomed, I trusted my Lord. I didn't have to be in charge of everything if I believed God stood guard on my behalf.

About the only thing I had to do was to find joy in the moment. I appreciated the little blessings showered upon my spirit, such as Easter dinner at my neighbors' house. Treasuring new companionship, I admired flecks of joy flying around the canvas of life. Guided and guarded by a loving Master Artist, I was becoming a piece of art.

Each brave move you make puts another artistic stroke on the print of your life. Dab your fingers in glorious colors and develop a new design. Don't worry if you're doing everything right or if all the lines are straight. Dare to add a few squiggles and purple polka dots.

Art is not only a good outlet for creativity, but it also can be therapeutic. A Window Between Worlds (AWBW) is a non-profit organization dedicated to using art to help end domestic violence.

AWBW sponsored an exhibit with the theme of pearls. Participants wrote down the irritant in their life, such as assault, and created a piece of art showing how to transform pain. Another display involved various people in a community, including law enforcement officials and family services representatives, to create a tree of life, with leaves and branches linking everyone who worked together to address family violence.[41]

Expressing yourself with art doesn't have to be expensive or elaborate. One shelter for battered women and children uses coloring books and crayons to provide an unobtrusive way to open communication and share stories.[42]

Art is a language that requires few words. Let it express your feelings. Give yourself permission to play with the enthusiasm of a little child, so caught up in the excitement of the moment that you have eyes only for the miracle unfolding before you.

Watch a lizard sunning or hop barefooted in mud puddles. Relax. When was the last time you tried to jump rope or play hopscotch? Above all, laugh.

Keep Firm Boundaries

Joy tastes sweet, but sometimes you have to set aside dessert to dine on dry staples, such as setting limits and keeping firm boundaries. You have to establish and maintain an area in which you feel safe. This involves not only physical protection, but emotional, as well. You determine what you need, make your expectations known, and hold people accountable for respecting your wishes.

If you don't establish a sturdy fence around what you value, you can get trampled.

I found this out when April rolled around. Five months had passed since Wendell and I separated. Steve and Luke visited my house from time to time, but the ruptured marriage put them in the middle of conflict. I struggled to maintain contact with them.

Luke called to say he would spend the night, but wanted to golf with friends after school.

"That'll be fine," I said. "Please check in by six o'clock for dinner because I have a meeting at seven."

He missed the meal, and I didn't know where he was. He hadn't called to explain the delay. A bit anxious but not alarmed, I went to my one-hour codependents' meeting. When I returned home, I saw a note Luke had left on the kitchen table saying he'd be back by nine o'clock.

Another hour slipped by, and I hadn't seen or heard from him. I worried, particularly when ambulances screamed up and down the road by the subdivision. Was Luke OK? Mixed with concern was an increasing irritation at his lack of consideration for how I might feel.

When he got in at ten o'clock, we argued.

"I've been worried. Where have you been?"

"I went with some friends. Didn't you see my note?"

"Yes, but that said you'd be home an hour ago, and it's a school night."

"Dad wouldn't treat me this way. He trusts me."

I had to set a boundary right away if I didn't want Luke coming and going however he pleased. I needed to show him that consideration for me mattered.

"Ambulances kept going by and I worried about you. I didn't know where you were or who you were with. If you're going to stay here, you have to follow certain rules, like don't take off unless I know where, and be home by nine."

Luke didn't like the boundaries, but I held my ground. He left the living room angry and went into his bedroom, slamming the door.

Wendell called before seven the next morning. "I'm returning Luke's call."

Luke must have phoned Wendell after the argument, without me knowing. I called Luke to the phone and left the room so they could talk privately.

I wanted Wendell to understand my concerns about accountability so Luke couldn't wander to whichever place offered greater freedom. So after Luke finished with the phone, I went to my bedroom and dialed Wendell.

I got a sleepy response from Steve.

"I'm trying to reach your dad."

"He's not here."

He'd just been talking to Luke. "Has he left for work?"

A pause ensued. "I don't know."

Steve's hesitation concerned me. "Are you saying Dad never came home last night?"

"No, he didn't."

Shock and sadness entered my heart with Steve's curt reply. I couldn't understand Wendell's behavior. What if there had been a medical emergency? Although Steve was a senior in high school and very responsible, he deserved better.

If the boys spent lots of time alone, no wonder Luke felt smothered with the guidelines I set. This scenario reinforced my concerns about the boys being safe with Wendell.

I also felt a spark of jealousy. Where had Wendell been all night? I chided myself for caring.

However, the conflict with Luke highlighted the changes in me. I felt confident establishing—and maintaining—healthy boundaries. I also practiced communicating my needs and expectations, instead of staying silent and holding resentment. And I didn't compromise my principles to appease Luke.

I discussed the situation with Reba after work that afternoon. She confirmed the boys weren't safe with Wendell, saying his narcissistic focus satisfied only his own desires.

"Your husband has betrayed you on many levels," Reba added.

"What do you mean?"

"When you said you needed time to heal, he refused to wait. Your faith and loyalty are attributes Wendell would use against you."

In years past, I had undercut or ignored my own judgment to preserve the marriage. By making an artificial peace, I often sacrificed what I needed. Now I practiced holding my position.

Affirmed by the session with Reba, I returned home around six o'clock to see Wendell helping Luke load his overnight bag into Wendell's trunk. Without begging or crying, I stood solid in the knowledge that I'd tried to do the right thing and would not facilitate their self-centeredness.

Before they drove away, I said in a calm tone, "Luke, I love you and I'm here for you. You're welcome back anytime, but the rules we spoke about will be in effect when you return."

I didn't know when Luke would come back or how often Wendell left the boys alone. I had no control over their choices. All I could do was walk a road of dignity, discovering the right course for me. The important thing was that I no longer made compromises that violated me.

Part of the challenge in healing from codependency is that you gave up boundaries long ago, so now you have trouble defining what area is yours and what belongs to others. Some shared space is OK, but each individual still must have his or her own territory.

Feelings of anger and sorrow indicate that boundaries have been crossed. Pay attention to these emotions to help identify places where you need to build better fences for protection.

Claiming your own territory takes practice. For example, a woman in her seventies found herself alone when the marriage to her high school sweetheart fell apart. She never had bought a car for herself because her husband always had taken care of that. She wanted a nice new car and went to a dealership to arrange a lease.

When she later realized the lease wasn't a good financial deal for her, she went back to the dealer and negotiated another arrangement. "I got myself into this mess, and I can get myself out of it," she said in a matter-of-fact tone.

Her can-do approach reflects the willingness to attempt tasks that used to seem too hard. The woman trusted her ability to haggle with the car salesperson, and she rallied to accomplish her mission, even if the effort required more than one trip. Her terrific attitude about learning shows that mistakes become building blocks for future successes when you practice direct communication and persist in having your needs met.

Healing Practice #7: Acquiring new skills boosts confidence to tackle more challenges.

God gives every person unique talents, and he wants you to use them. When you step out in faith and practice with what he's already provided, you'll soon discover how much more he will entrust to you.

Study Questions

1. Start a journal about a new project you'd like to tackle. What fears keep you from trying? Make a self-improvement date for this week. What will you do to expand confidence and gain new skills?

2. How do you handle your anger? Do you let it get mushy like a rotten banana and keep it inside? Or do you express concerns in a calm tone when the time is ripe?

3. Holidays, anniversaries, and birthdays can trigger emotions without you being aware. Look at your calendar and schedule special activities around days that might otherwise get lost in sad memories.

4. How have you seen children used by an adult to manipulate or control another adult? What can be done to protect the children?

5. What "buddy systems" exist in your life? Who has given you the gift of encouragement?

6. Instead of waiting around for someone to help you up, watch for people to whom you can give hope. A simple word of encouragement from you to a tired store clerk could make a huge difference in that person's day—and yours.

7. Imagine filling helium balloons with all your anger, unforgiveness, and bitterness. Tie the bottoms with string, then release the strands. Watch the wind catch the balloons and carry them higher and farther away. Soon, you can only make out tiny dots. Smile at the relief that comes from letting go of pain you no longer need to carry.

8. Think of titles that would sum up the recovery themes in this chapter. Two examples of crazy paraphrases might be "Sitting on your bottom results in hemorrhoids" or "If you want to swing like Tarzan, you have to climb a tree." Have some fun with this!

Resources

Codependents Anonymous sponsors meetings throughout the nation for people who want to develop healthy relationships. The CoDA website also has a list of patterns and characteristics of codependents. For more information, go to http://www.coda.org/.

A Window Between Worlds (AWBW) is a nonprofit organization dedicated to using art to help end domestic violence. Since 1991, AWBW has provided creative expression as a healing tool for more 49,500 battered women and their children in crisis shelters, transitional homes, and outreach centers throughout the United States. To learn more about the program, visit the website at www.awbw.org, call 310-396-0317 x210 or send e-mail to info@awbw.org.

CHAPTER EIGHT

CERTAIN OF GOD'S LOVE

As you more clearly define what territory is yours and know you are capable of defending it with God's help, you will be more comfortable inviting others to spaces you'd like to share. You'll have a better feel for who is trustworthy, and you'll recognize more quickly when someone is trespassing in an area you don't want them.

This ability to see definite property lines frees you from the uncertainty you used to deal with when you tiptoed everywhere, feeling like a trespasser anyplace you walked. Feeling certain of God's love empowers you to claim open, lush fields for yourself. You no longer will settle for arid pieces of desert with a cactus or two.

By late spring, I felt ready to include others in the sanctuary I'd found. Creating invitations for a costume-jewelry party, I saw this as an opportunity to welcome friends to my new residence. I drove to the old neighborhood, wondering how people would respond to my long absence and marital separation.

I'd left almost five months before without saying much to anyone due to my embarrassment about the marital separation. I didn't think anyone would believe me about the problems with Wendell; he presented such a respectable outward appearance. How could others fully comprehend the pain I'd hidden so carefully and had trouble admitting, even to myself?

Because many batterers do not have criminal records, it is often only the intimate partners who see and experience the abusers' seething rage.[43] Outside the immediate family, the batterer usually has a reputation for being a hard worker, a good parent, and a responsible citizen.[44]

Would my former neighbors and friends want to be around me or would they shun me for leaving my family?

I was pleasantly surprised by how warmly I was received. Neighbors asked how I was doing and gave me hugs. On one front porch, a married couple sat with me as we sipped ginger ale, catching up.

"You look good," Jimmy told me.

His compliment surprised me, especially since I was wearing workout clothes and had my hair in a ponytail. "I just came from the gym." I didn't *feel* pretty.

"You've got your sparkle back," he said, looking me in the eyes.

His wife, Julie, nodded in agreement.

What a blessing! He wasn't looking at the outside; he saw the peacefulness in my soul. His comment assured me that despite the pain of separation and losing the kids, something wonderful had happened with the healing of my spirit. Somehow, I had climbed out of the pit of anger and despair, finding a place of contentment that reflected in my face.

What allowed the inner light to shine? I wasn't sure. Maybe knowing Wendell would never be faithful freed me to accept the death of the marriage. But the real reason for the sparkle was the knowledge that God loved me, that my friends liked me, and that I could find my way forward, even without Wendell.

The time had arrived to put away the notion that I could save my marriage. I conducted a wedding-ring-retirement ceremony, tying my gold band and diamond ring together with a pale blue ribbon and placing them in my jewelry box. I got out other pieces of colorful costume jewelry to adorn myself with.

At the codependents' meeting that night, I flashed my fake bling.

"You have a lot more strength than you think you have," said a sixty-nine-year-old woman nicknamed Lil D. She had inner beauty that radiated with peace. Her sweet face, wreathed by a fluffy white halo of hair, featured a warm smile. I wanted to be like her, with an attractiveness not from makeup, clothing, or jewelry, but from the certainty that God valued and loved her.

Living in an abusive partnership drains your self-esteem. It takes a while to build up confidence. When you start to experience that peaceful feeling, you'll know the healing process is progressing. You won't have solutions to all the problems, but you will know that God is empowering you to face each hurdle with grace and competence.

Seeking Education about Dysfunctional Relationships

As you stand tall and explore new ground, you'll want to learn more about dysfunctional relationships so that you can identify, and dodge, pitfalls.

Your family of origin often establishes what your expectations are for love, but those early experiences might limit healthy possibilities. Take time to investigate how poor communication and inadequate strategies for resolving conflict impact your ability to be in wholesome partnerships.

As I gradually accepted that my marriage with Wendell couldn't be repaired, I considered spending life as a single woman. Although the thought didn't terrify me as it once had, I wondered if I would ever have someone with whom to share my life. How could I trust my judgment after spending so many years in an unhealthy partnership? What could I do differently to keep from falling into another bad arrangement?

God again provided unexpected resources, this time through a new Sunday school class called "How to Avoid Destructive Relationships." Two men facilitated the instruction: one was a teacher who'd retired from the Federal Bureau of Investigation after profiling serial killers and negotiating hostage releases, and the other mediated contract negotiations between large corporations and employees. These were not your typical Bible study leaders.

A crowd filled the room during the first session. One leader said statistics showed that one in three women will be sexually assaulted in her lifetime and that one in six boys will be sexually assaulted by the age of eighteen.[45] He added that both women and men could be abusers and that abusive relationships develop over time, though there are early warning signs.

The instructors shared research conducted by Dr. Joseph M. Carver, a clinical psychologist in private practice in southern Ohio. Dr. Carver identified twenty behaviors that often signal an abusive relationship, and his checklist included the following.

Warning Signs of an Abusive Relationship

1. Abusers treat people roughly. They may hurt someone physically (such as pinching, shoving, or hitting), or they may break others' treasured possessions.

2. Abusers make quick attachments and often say "I love you" early on in a brand-new relationship. They realize that their ability to connect emotionally is shallow, so they assert control quickly.

3. Abusers have frightening tempers. They blow up easily and make threats. They may mistreat animals. Even if this temper isn't initially directed toward a partner, violence can turn on anyone nearby.

4. Abusers kill other people's self-confidence by always correcting them. Others are afraid of making mistakes or saying the wrong thing, so they walk on eggshells to avoid conflict.

5. Abusers cut off support networks of family, friends, and coworkers. They seek to become the sole frame of reference and use isolation as a form of control.

6. Abusers have a "mean/sweet" cycle. They intentionally do something hurtful, such as not showing up for a date, then do all the sweet things they did early in the dating relationship. The abused individual hangs on in hopes that this is the end of the cycle. But with each repetition, self-confidence erodes and the abused party's ability for self-defense is reduced.

7. Abusers say, "It's your fault," never taking personal responsibility. This can become an unconscious lifestyle for them.

8. Abusers panic if a breakup is looming. They may cry and plead if their partner tries to leave. They might threaten suicide, going back to old lovers, quitting jobs, etc. All of these drastic outcomes would then be the "fault" of the abused partner.

9. Abusers often enlist the help of friends or family to pressure their partner into maintaining the status quo. They consider the person held under their influence as a "prized possession," and they work tirelessly to contain their prey.

10. Abusers don't allow outside interests. They don't want their partners to have any activities that could be a source of support.

11. Abusers keep track of the abused at all times. They want to know everyone their partner talks to and about what. They keep close tabs on where the abused person goes.

12. Abusers publicly embarrass their partner. They make disparaging comments in front of others to humiliate the abused and also use verbal intimidation.

13. Abusers are never satisfied. One person can't possibly do everything they desire.

14. Abusers have a sense of entitlement. Others owe them—just because.

15. Over time, family and friends notice the abused partner's withdrawal. When they confront the abuser or the abused, the abuser prevents family or friends from visiting.

16. Abusers frequently talk about violence or fights. Constant confrontation may become the abused person's lifestyle.

17. Abusers seem to have two distinct personalities. The abused never knows which one needs to be dealt with. Most healthy people act consistently and have a uniform representation.

18. Abusers often have friends that the abused doesn't like.

19. Abusers discount the opinions and feelings of others. They'll tell anyone who disagrees that the other person is emotionally disturbed.

20. Abusers make life crazy. Even nonviolent people will start yelling and screaming after spending time with an abuser because they can't take the craziness anymore.[46]

Seventeen of these descriptors applied to Wendell. Finally, I had words for the gut-level reactions I hadn't known before how to substantiate.

Even while dating Wendell in college, upsetting events had foreshadowed problems. I ignored the warning signs, hoping love would solve everything. But when I was really honest with myself, I had to admit that I silenced my misgivings because that was easier than being alone.

When you look at the list of warning signs, do you recognize similar behavior in the person you love? Credible outside sources, such as counseling professionals and church leaders, confirm that identifiable patterns make up abuse. Are you surprised to hear your story in their checklist?

This means that many other people have gone through the struggles you face and have found a way to heal. How can you use this information to protect yourself or someone else?

Practicing Respectful Conflict Resolution

Armed with a heightened awareness about the patterns of dysfunction, you'll have the insight to see developing problems sooner. Use this newfound knowledge to test arrangements and make sure they are good for you. Listen to the inner voice that alerts you to potentially uncomfortable situations. Heed any warnings and act to let others know where you stand and what you expect.

I was able to practice these skills in my own life the next week at Sunday school. The occasion began when the leader asked members why they attended the class on destructive relationships. After several folks shared very personal situations,

I noticed the leader fingering a miniature microphone clipped to his collar.

Surprised, I raised my hand. "Is this being recorded?"

"Yes. We're making a teaching tape for those who can't attend."

"I wasn't told about that, and I'm not comfortable with what I shared leaving this room." I tried to assess how the others felt, but no one would meet my gaze. They all remained silent.

"I can erase your comments," the leader said as he walked to the computer.

Although I appreciated having a church family and had benefited from this fellowship, I didn't like the idea that the leaders hadn't even considered the courtesy of informing us first, particularly when the course centered on a sensitive topic.

Who might hear those tapes? Some of my high school students attended this church, and I wanted to protect my privacy.

"I'm not trying to be difficult," I said. "But isn't taping without disclosure illegal?"

Other attendees shifted in their seats. I didn't want to be rude, so I let the issue drop.

After class, I approached the instructor privately. "I'm sorry to have caused a fuss. But I want to feel safe in a church class and know that my information is kept private."

He couldn't understand why I felt violated, and that bothered me even more. I left to go to the service, but the unresolved issue still irritated me. What happened to people too shy to stand up for themselves? Had the church leadership fully considered this taping policy? I wrote my concerns on a prayer card addressed to the elders and placed it in the offering basket.

A week went by with no response.

Finally the class leader called me at home, wanting to discuss why I felt so strongly about the taping.

"For someone to attend a class about abusive relationships is huge. It's like coming out of the closet. People in that situation need to be able to share, without worrying about how their private comments might later be used."

"Oh. I hadn't thought about that."

"What if secondhand information got back to an abuser? Then the victim's efforts to find help would backfire and could end up harming him or her."

"I see what you mean. I apologize."

"Educational tapes on such a sensitive topic are a good idea, but you need to offer signed consent forms so all participants know the arrangement from the beginning."

"Thanks for sharing your concerns," he said. "I hadn't thought about this from your point of view. We've taped almost twenty sessions, and you're the first person to bring this to light."

As unpleasant as confronting concerns is, it can have positive results. I had stood up for what was important to me; the leader heard my ideas and responded with an acceptable compromise. Isn't that what healthy relationships are about?

If you have been in situations in the past in which conflict became violent, you probably tend to avoid anything that could cause disagreement. You make no sound and become invisible. These survival techniques don't help you grow in new relationships. With emerging safety, you must be willing to change how you deal with issues.

Any time two people connect, there is bound to be a difference of opinion somewhere along the way. Arguments occur, but they don't have to involve screaming or hitting. To be an equal partner—whether at work, in a friendship, or in romantic relationships—you must exercise your power and voice your needs. Do so with respect and expect to be heard. This paves the way for people to negotiate what they need and reach a mutually satisfying agreement.

As you become more assured of yourself, you'll find that your voice gets bolder and clearer. Like singing with a choir, practicing direct communication makes your vocal muscles stronger and can result in wonderful harmony.

Speaking up for things you want and need feels so good after years of being silent. You'll find others to be much more responsive when they know you will stand your ground for a reasonable request. It takes a while to feel comfortable asking for something after years being neglected or told what you want doesn't matter, but keep working to express yourself.

There's no reason to feel guilty about saying you want something. That's not being selfish or self-centered; it is being in touch with yourself and knowing what you need. Many people find that directness refreshing because it removes guessing games and eliminates confusion in relationships.

Receiving Forgiveness

While you practice speaking up, also tune your ears to hear better. As the loud noises of criticism and complaint about your shortcomings get quieted with the absence of an abusive partner, let God's tender whispers of encouragement fill your mind.

The Lord will tell you that he knows how hard you've tried to make everything right. He understands your pain over the marriage's failure. He'll sooth your anxiety as you wonder if there's more you should have done to please him and everyone else.

God will let you know that he loves you as you are. He doesn't fault you for the disintegration of a partnership that requires two people working toward reconciliation. God knows you have done all that you can right now. Listen for his assurances that you are loved and forgiven for any flaws. His soothing voice will come at unexpected times and places.

Traveling with a group of women from church, I attended a May conference at an ocean resort. The speaker shared the story of her marriage that ended after twenty-nine years. Describing her life after divorce, she said it was like riding a boat along the sea. A sudden explosion destroyed the ship, and she fell into the water. She said she hung on to pieces of wreckage, but God told her to let go of the debris because he would save her.

The woman added that sometimes God must pry away our fingers, which are desperately grasping for control. She quoted Proverbs 3:5: "Trust in the Lord with all your heart and lean not on your own understanding; in all your ways acknowledge him, and he will make your paths straight."

Will you trust God to lead you beyond brokenness to hidden treasures?

Walking alone on the beach in the afternoon, I thought about my losses. What would have been my twenty-first wedding anniversary with Wendell had passed in silent oblivion. Anger and bitterness tempted me, but my desire for healing was more powerful. Facing a chilly wind, I listened to the timeless pounding of the surf. I wanted God to take my debris and construct a new platform.

The Lord had a plan and destiny for me, but I needed to release the broken pieces clutched in my hands to reach for the good he offered. Watching waves surge onto the shore made me think about the constancy of God's love. Emotions tumbled in my mind, emerging as a poem.

The Treasure Hunt

Going on a treasure hunt within the frothy foam
Wading around tangled seaweed
Fragments of me.

Black leather mermaid's purse
Plastic pink octopus
Shells shattered under pressure
Just like me.
Wind tugs at my hood while memories pull at my heart.
It's painful to go back to the start.
Old hurts swirl and surface, laying claim;
Imprisoning the future, twisted in blame.

But God's voice rumbled,
"Come back to me, little one.
"I will make you whole
"and mend the rips in your soul."

Dunes piled high on hidden regrets
Drifted away, guilt edged in crimson,
Deposited in a holy bank, forgiven.

Rays of Sonlight whispered, "Don't give up yet.
"I have more for you than you can believe.
"Sheltered, shielded within my love.
"Tiny flecks of sand, carefully arranged,
"Each for a purpose, each for a stand.
"Watch for the movement of my hand.
"Nothing's impossible.
"Just watch me.
"After all, didn't I make the sea?"

The words to this poem had flowed forth almost effortlessly, as though God himself was chanting the encouragement. He seemed to tell me that regardless of my past mistakes, he could redeem my current circumstances.

He can do the same in your life. Piling up regrets accomplishes nothing. You need to know that God washes us clean as the tide sweeps shore each day. There's no need to look for broken bits and pieces when he wants to bring treasures.

Just as the woman speaking at the conference used her life experience to comfort others, so too can you develop compassion and wisdom. God will smooth the rough edges of your shell to reveal intricate patterns of forgiveness and grace.

Banishing Guilty Feelings

Charting a course to circumnavigate deep regrets requires clarity of mind. You don't need to keep dragging a buoy marker of guilt; that will only exhaust you. Instead, acknowledge what you might have done differently and commit to making better choices in the future. Don't beat yourself up for past mistakes.

I must have asked myself a million times whether there was anything else I should have done to save my marriage and protect the boys.

My attorney, Hattie, had requested a timeline about the marriage to prepare documents for the custody hearing. I retrieved old diaries from the closet, which I had begun years ago to keep track of events, since Wendell often told me I didn't remember anything accurately. As I read these records, I couldn't believe how many painful instances I'd managed to forget until I had to look at the full sequence of events penned during eight years of personal writing.

For example, Wendell didn't like dealing with financial records, so we had filed one year's tax return late, without an extension. He also ran up credit card debt into the thousands of dollars, without me knowing. Another time, I found out accidentally that he had taken an advance on the equity line of credit on our home. His lack of honest disclosure destroyed my ability to trust him.

Whenever I confronted Wendell about an issue, things would get ugly. Although he only physically attacked me twice, this possibility always hovered in my subconscious. Sometimes Wendell gave the silent treatment for several days, or he slept in another room.

These memories made the old feelings of abandonment and rejection resurface. No wonder I'd felt worn out and lost. But now, with the benefit of distance and safety, I saw how I'd blocked most of the unpleasantness to maintain the marriage. Maybe selective memory constituted a survival skill, or perhaps I'd been too weak for anything but avoidance.

In retrospect, I'm glad I started those diaries. Keeping a journal is a good way to recognize and record feelings. If you don't keep a diary already, you should start one, even if it's in a simple notebook. Reviewing the writing for trends every month or so will help you see where you are making progress and how God answers prayers.

Patterns revealed in my journals showed my repeated compromises, but each retreat led to a deeper hole in which I got buried. A growing awareness about our checkered past, rather than the idealized version I usually chose to see, helped me overcome lingering doubts about the current measures I was taking to change my life.

Another source of relief from guilt came at the end of May, during the final Sunday school class on abusive relationships. Instead of the typical advice to give unconditional love no matter what, Pastor Wayne used biblical stories about King Saul to offer practical tips for protecting oneself from an abuser.

"Saul was an impressive young man God chose to govern the people," the pastor said. "However, Saul had a rash nature and failed to remain humble before the Lord. Soon, insecurity and envy drove him to consider killing his own family members." (See 1 Samuel 10–14.)

Like Saul, Wendell had many good qualities, such as leadership, but he often misused his power for selfish gain.

I could barely take notes fast enough to copy the information into my journal as Pastor Wayne described three stages of abusive behavior originally outlined by Lenore Walker in 1979.[47] Pastor Wayne applied Walker's Cycle of Violence theory to behaviors revealed by Saul toward David:[48]

1. Honeymoon Stage. Saul invited David to live in the royal palace, where David served as a musician and received privileges.
2. Abuse Stage: In a fit of jealousy, Saul tried to kill David. "Saul had a spear in his hand and he hurled it, saying to himself, 'I'll pin David to the wall.' But David eluded him twice" (1 Samuel 18:10–11).
3. Makeup Stage: To apologize for his attack, Saul gave David new gifts and honors. "Saul was afraid of David, because the Lord was with David but had left Saul. So Saul sent David away and gave him command over a

thousand men" (1 Samuel 18:12–13).

I could relate to David's experiences with Saul. Wendell also had made grand gestures, such as planning elaborate vacations, but I could never predict his fits of anger. What should a godly person do in such confusing circumstances? Gripping my pen, I waited for the minister's advice about how to react to someone's dangerous behavior.

Pastor Wayne identified five appropriate ways that David responded to Saul's abuse:

1. He left the abusive situation (1 Samuel 19:10).

2. He refused to be lulled back to King Saul through tears and resolutions, without Saul's demonstrated change of heart and behavior (1 Samuel 26:21–25).

3. He sought help from the Philistines, who were stronger than Saul (1 Samuel 27:4).

4. He used hardship for self-examination. He sought advice from a wise counselor who had a vested interest in seeing both points of view. David asked for advice from Jonathan, who was Saul's son as well as David's close friend (1 Samuel 20:1–23).

5. He did not remain bitter. Despite suffering, David kept his heart tender to show Saul kindness and respect (1 Samuel 24:1–15; 2 Samuel 1:17–24).

Pastor Wayne's insights comforted me, and reaffirmed my decision about leaving Wendell. Having a scriptural foundation for setting boundaries refreshed me. I also realized these protective steps could be applied to any relationship; the connection didn't have to be romantic.

Biblical precedent justified removing myself from a harmful situation. This Old Testament story didn't negate the "forgive-seven-times-seventy" principle of the New Testament; however, forgiving someone and hanging around for more battering were two different things.

The pastor closed his message by mentioning biblical examples of abusers who healed with God's help. These included Moses, who murdered an Egyptian, and John, a "Son of Thunder" who came to be known as the disciple of love.

One modern-day former batterer and recovering alcoholic confessed the grief he felt when he realized how he'd harmed his spouse. "I woke up one morning and rolled over to look at my wife. Her arms were covered in bruises from what I'd done to her the night before. I broke down and cried. I knew I had to change."

The Domestic Abuse Intervention Programs, mentioned in chapters one and six, also help men who batter. "We developed the leading curriculum for facilitators of men's groups," said Linda Riddle, DAIP executive director. "We conduct international trainings and work with about 250 men here in Duluth every year."

According to Ms. Riddle, a decade-long study revealed that male batterers who completed DAIP's twenty-seven-week class did not get rearrested for domestic violence in 77 percent of the cases.[49]

Those transformations offered hope for Wendell, if he asked God to assist him, but Wendell had to choose his own journey. My attempts to control and manipulate—even for reasonable causes—did no good. Releasing the notion that I could change Wendell, I realized that withdrawing to protect myself did not make me dishonorable or disloyal.

You, too, can release feelings of guilt that tie you in knots but take you nowhere. You did the best you could with what you knew at the time, but now you are older and wiser. You have the strength to make better choices, and you will.

Healing Practice #8: Overcome weakness by doing your homework.

Regular weight lifting builds strong muscles and a fit body. In the same way, facing fears will empower you to grow in wisdom and competence.

Study Questions

1. Look in your jewelry box. What memories do those precious objects contain? If the box is empty, what can you do to decorate yourself? Don't focus on cost, but on symbols of what you hold dear in life. For some, butterfly pendants symbolize rebirth and hope. For others, a necklace represents the way we are linked to others. Invest time to discover what makes you feel valued.

2. Think about Dr. Carver's warning signs for potentially abusive relationships. Look up the full article at http://www. drjoecarver.com/clients/49355/File/IdentifyingLosers.html. Do any of these descriptors characterize your marriage or other relationships?

3. Should a church official or Bible study leader tape a class without informing the participants? Explain your answer. If you discovered someone doing that, what would you do?

4. Identify debris you're clinging to, such as anger, that keeps you from moving forward. Release these to God. Ask for help in trusting him more.

5. Pastor Wayne gave a scriptural basis for five steps of dealing with abusive relationships. Write these steps on a piece of paper. Then write out your ideas for how to apply this teaching to your situation.

Resources

For more information about Lenore Walker's Cycle of Violence theory, go to http://ezinearticles.com/?Lenore-Walkers-Cycle-of-Violence&id=1366375 or to http://www.webster.edu/~woolflm/walker2.html.

Reading poetry can help you find words for intense emotions. "Invictus" by William Ernest Henry, encourages a person to overcome adversity. That piece served as an inspirational theme in the movie about Nelson Mandela cast with Morgan Freeman. You can choose to be the "master of your fate." The poem's full text can be found at http://www.poemhunter.com/poem/invictus.

Look for other poems that speak to you. Emily Dickinson's "Hope is the thing with feathers" can be found at http://academic.brooklyn.cuny.edu/english/melani/cs6/hope.html. Consider writing your own poetry to explore your feelings.

STAGE THREE:

SAFE ON SHORE

You stand firm in your unique identity, staying involved in healthy fellowship with God and other people.

CHAPTER NINE

DODGING TEMPTATION

From the deep waters of terror and doubt, you swim through shark-infested zones of anger and guilt until shallow turquoise waves gently push you toward a beautiful shore. Knowing a loving God accepts you—without condition—helps you establish yourself on solid ground. You don't have to strain anymore. You can sun yourself on the shore of his steadfastness and rest secure that no matter what else might happen, God is in control and will care for you.

Riding out the tidal waves of change makes you stronger. You know now that you have an inner strength that makes you a force to be contended with. You carry yourself with a quiet composure that commands respect.

You no longer identify yourself as a victim, nor do you limit yourself to the label of survivor.[50] You grow to embrace an image of yourself that expands beyond the heartache you've endured to see an attractive, capable, and interesting person who has much to offer. You feel comfortable with yourself and celebrate having autonomy, anticipating good things ahead.

Having accepted that divorce appeared more likely than reconciliation, I mentally straddled the strange world of not being married, but not being single either. After months of separation, my mind-set changed from "How can I heal the marriage?" to "How do I move on?"

Would I find real love? What I'd thought was love before had been so hurtful. How could I invest in another relationship, wondering the whole time if we shared the same values? I didn't want to take an impulsive action that I'd regret.

Summer approached, and I wanted to line up a second job to keep me busy when school finished. A friend introduced me to Paulette, a nice British lady who owned a floral shop. Paulette hired me on a trial basis one weekend to help decorate at an outdoor wedding.

At the site of the ceremony, bright red geraniums bloomed around the patio. Sunshine danced on a nearby river where ducks coasted on the current.

Working in the heat made us thirsty. As Paulette and I lugged arrangements around, we noticed a member of the wedding party cutting fruit for the reception at the bar. Yummy yellow pineapples and deep red strawberries looked tempting. We'd started work early, and had skipped breakfast.

"Those grapes sure look good," Paulette said in a louder-than-necessary voice.

Almost instantly, a handsome, dark-haired man appeared beside us, holding a tray with freshly sliced treats. "My name is Tom. Help yourselves."

I pondered whether I should eat while working, particularly when the food belonged to the bride. While I hesitated, my boss smiled and plopped frosty pieces of fruit in her mouth, so I did too. The tart grapes cooled my tongue as I glanced over at the handsome guy who had given them to me.

Soon after, Tom and I began a game of tag. Right after I'd put an arrangement on a table, he'd walk beside me to set out napkins and cutlery. Tom's apparent interest in me was flattering, but it also frightened me.

The setting of a wedding to meet someone new seemed ironic. I had just entered the seventh month of my marital separation. But Wendell was already dating other women, and loneliness bothered me. Wasn't I free to enjoy myself too?

"How do you like working with a florist?" Tom asked.

"I don't know. Today's my first day. During the week, I teach high school."

Feeling terribly rusty at flirting, I dug in the bucket filled with blue hydrangeas, peonies, white roses, and yellow ivy. Tom murmured something about getting ice, then wandered off to help the groom.

As Tom talked with friends, I busied myself near the pavilion. Listening as I worked, I wondered if Tom was trustworthy.

The bridegroom's black dog ran up to me, holding a red Frisbee in its mouth and wagging its tail. I tugged the toy free and threw. Unfortunately, I had poor aim, and the disc landed in a high branch overhanging the river.

I looked around to see if anyone had observed my error. To my embarrassment, Tom made eye contact. He shrugged, but he didn't attempt to rescue the dog's toy. No one else seemed to notice. I stifled a laugh, and hoped the dog would forgive me.

Tom approached. "Are you coming back tonight for the ceremony?"

"No, I'm only here to help Paulette." I moved toward the van to unload more supplies. He watched me, but didn't say anything.

I wistfully imagined wearing a sexy dress and dancing in a man's close embrace. Then I quickly rejected that fantasy. I couldn't make my first marriage work; I wasn't even divorced yet. Didn't I have a moral obligation to be faithful to my vow to honor my husband, at least until a judge said otherwise?

I couldn't give myself permission to date, and not just on legal grounds. Grief over the death of my marriage still held me. I also had a lot to learn about myself. I needed to search my heart for answers about past choices before I got distracted with another man.

Unless my heart healed fully and my understanding of my value to God deepened, I would repeat the same dysfunctional patterns with other men. Hadn't fears of inadequacy pushed me toward Wendell in the beginning? I had to prove I could stand on my own two feet.

Within an hour, Paulette and I completed the floral designs. As we left the wedding site, Tom opened the gate for us and waved good-bye.

I was proud of myself for trying a new job and avoiding a romantic complication.

Paulette called the next day. "Thank you so much for helping."

"It was my pleasure. That place was beautiful."

"Actually, business isn't the main reason I called. Tom phoned last night, asking for your number. I wanted to check with you to see if that was OK."

I didn't want to review personal drama with a part-time employer. "I've been separated from my husband a few months, and my emotions are still raw. I don't want to give out my number."

"Oh, I didn't realize your pain was so fresh," Paulette said. "Tom left his numbers for work and home. If you like, I can give them to you, in case you want to call him later."

Not wanting to be rude, I jotted down the numbers, wondering if I was losing my mind. What was I doing? I couldn't call some guy yet. I wasn't divorced! "Would you please tell Tom I'm flattered but not available? I'm vulnerable now and need time to heal."

"I'll tell him. And I'll ring you next time I'm arranging flowers. After all, you haven't had a chance to do centerpieces yet."

After thanking her, I hung up. Tom's phone numbers stared at me from the notepad, and I felt weak. To avoid temptation, I shredded the paper into little bits. Then I put the scraps in the kitchen wastebasket, under rotten lettuce in case I changed my mind.

None of these precautions had anything to do with Tom. I wanted a clear conscience. The marriage had to be officially dissolved before I saw someone else.

Maybe other people would scoff at this old-fashioned ideal of fidelity, but I had to be true to my principles. Besides, fleeing one bad relationship and running into the arms of another man only complicated matters. Escapism would have prevented me from taking a hard look at myself and distracted me from doing what I needed to grow. My goal was not to find another man, but to rebuild and rediscover myself with a fuller awareness of how much God loved me.

Still, the temptation of Tom's interest tasted delicious.

Loneliness can tempt you to compromise your goals. Be careful not to seek approval from other partners until you are confident in yourself. If you pursue other relationships prematurely, you will most likely repeat old patterns and choose someone just like the person you are trying to move on from. The unconscious dance of dominance and dependency will haunt you if you don't take time to firmly establish yourself in healthy independence.

Identifying Patterns

Hone your recovery behaviors with non-romantic relationships, such as with friends or co-workers. Look for opportunities to better understand how you react to stress or resolve conflict since your spouse no longer consumes all your attention. Keep exercising your ability to voice your thoughts and needs.

Practice applying what you've learned about yourself and healthy behavior to each new circumstance. Quickly handle any weakness that could limit your progress.

Train your eye to see situations that duplicate issues you've faced in the past. Be prepared to react positively with your new skills and insight. Imagine yourself cleaning house, where you put everything in emotional order and tidy up.

Tidying up is exactly what I found myself doing shortly after my flower-arranging stint; my parents were visiting the next day, and I wanted my home spotless. They were staying with me for the weekend to celebrate Steve's graduation from high school.

To prepare for their visit, I dusted the extra bedroom. It was there that something caught my eye; tucked by the mirror on the dresser's corner rested a tiny piece of folded notebook paper, labeled "XX" in Luke's handwriting. Luke had removed all of his other things in March. Had he left behind a love note that I'd just now noticed?

Unfolding the sheet of paper, I saw *February 21* scribbled in Luke's handwriting, followed by the title of an X-rated movie. My expectation of XXOO turned into *Oh, my goodness!* Why would Luke have hidden a copy of that title and date?

Uncertain of what to do, I placed the note in my desk drawer and made a mental note to discuss the matter with my lawyer later. I finished cleaning the house, but still felt dirty after the unsettling images the note provoked.

The next morning, classroom activities consumed me until noon, when I left to meet my parents for lunch at a restaurant near my school. A delicious aroma of baked cheeses and basil greeted me in the Italian place, as did my parents' warm hugs.

Dad and Mom looked good, and I appreciated them making the long trip to celebrate Steve's achievement. I also felt glad they would be present to help buffer me from Wendell.

"Would anyone like a glass of wine?" the waiter asked.

Dad fidgeted, fiddled with the menu, set down the wine list, then said, "No."

Moments later when the waiter returned, Dad said, "I want a glass of wine after all."

Since when did Dad drink at lunch?

Later, in the ladies' restroom, I asked Mom, "Is Dad drinking every day?"

"Yes, but he doesn't have as much when I'm around."

"Mom, you're kidding yourself. If he's drinking at all, it's a systemic disease."

As soon as the words left my mouth, I regretted them. Sorrow shadowed Mom's face. I loved my parents and felt protective toward them. I wanted to share what I was learning about alcoholism and help them find a way out of destructive patterns. The problem was, my blunt delivery attacked my mother's ability to hear.

With an apologetic tone, I said, "Mom, I admire your loyalty and caring. I just don't want to see you get dragged down."

Every bit of energy she had invested in supervising him had drained her of the ability to pursue her own interests and development. In my parents' relationship, I saw a mirror image of my marriage to Wendell, and that revelation appalled me. I didn't want my parents to settle for a mediocre arrangement that frustrated them both and left them unfulfilled. By sharing insights candidly, I hoped to serve as a catalyst for change, but speaking up involved risk. Would I alienate them? They hadn't asked for my input. Was I being disloyal to my father?

The scenario resembled seeing an approaching high-speed vehicle, with an unsuspecting pedestrian in the road. Didn't danger merit yelling a warning? If so, why did I feel like a traitor?

My parents epitomized the classic codependent cycle. As Mom became more protective of Dad, she lost more of herself. Dad wrestled with the disease but didn't think he had a problem because he ran several successful businesses. My attempts to discuss concerns annoyed him, and alcohol and its effects created a barrier between us. Shattering the illusion that everything was all right would bring them pain.

You may notice similar indicators of trouble in your family of origin as you learn more about alcoholism and abuse. Exploring your past with new eyes often uncovers the matching sock that's been hidden at the bottom of the dirty laundry basket for a long time.

In your excitement about newfound knowledge, you'll probably want to share what you've discovered, but be sure to exercise caution; speaking up requires tact.

Remember how you wanted to keep your problems private early in recovery? You wanted to protect your spouse and yourself from ridicule. Well, others feel the same way. They might be reluctant to hear the truth spoken out loud. Encouraging change is admirable, but people must choose their own time to face the pain of addictions. Honor your convictions but also respect their right to refuse your insights.

Strong love existed between my parents and me. They knew genuine concern motivated my actions. They also wanted to support Steve, Luke, and me. However, unresolved issues overshadowed what should have been a joy-filled celebration. Wendell complicated matters by inviting my parents—but not me—to his house that Friday night for a graduation party.

Earlier in the week Steve had asked me not to go, saying he wanted to avoid any chance of conflict. I respected his wishes. I didn't want to cause tension on a night he should be able to relax and be happy.

That evening, I sat alone, feeling dejected. When Dad and Mom returned from the party, they tried to console me.

On Saturday morning, I dressed in the black gown and cap faculty wore. At least Wendell couldn't keep me from giving Steve his diploma today. According to staff tradition at our school, I would stand onstage and hand the certificate to Steve. I gripped the paper in my left hand so I could shake with my right hand.

I didn't want to embarrass Steve by crying or kissing him. But as soon as Steve's hand touched mine to get the paper, he pulled me into a tight bear hug. I treasured that moment, knowing Steve's love for me remained strong.

Steve's embrace declared his support. Savoring that healing knowledge throughout the weekend made saying good-bye to Dad and Mom easier.

After they left, I sat at home, overcome by emotions. How could time have passed so quickly? It seemed like just a moment before that Steve was playing on the kitchen floor with "wheel-pops," his name for Matchbox cars. Now Steve drove a 1978 Chevy truck that Wendell had lovingly helped him restore. How much more precious time would be lost before Luke graduated too?

By Monday, depression loomed. I took out Steve's baby book and pasted the graduation picture of us onstage on the last page. Tears of loss welled up.

Then I gave myself a pep talk. *No one has died or been diagnosed with cancer. You have a safe home and enough money to pay the bills. Your kids are healthy and succeeding. You have family who cares about you. Steve is moving into another stage of life, but he still loves you.*

Steve was ready for the challenges of college. I needed to let him go and trust that God would guide him.

Please, Lord, bring Luke back to me too.

Even when you are in the stage of being safe on shore, life still happens. You'll face difficulties and disappointments. Healing comes in fits and starts; you won't achieve all that you want immediately. You'll have to accept some uncertainty, knowing not all issues will be solved right away.

What gets you through this is the same thing that gave you breath while drowning and kept you swimming against all the odds: your trust in God. Just as he has brought you to a place of safety and rest, he'll guide the ones you love. The best thing you can do for them is to continue to progress yourself. That affirms for everyone that patterns can be broken and more possibilities exist.

Knowing God as Friend

While you may endure silence because of others' unwillingness to listen to what you have to say, God wants to be with you. He looks forward to hearing your ideas and welcomes your candor. He doesn't fear the times when your hope flags or your optimism crashes.

As a loving parent, the Lord wants to share in your life. He treasures time with you. He holds each second in your company as precious and awaits your invitation to be together.

In a similar manner, I looked for opportunities to be with Steve as the summer raced by and he prepared for college. He arranged to meet me downtown at our favorite old-time diner for peanut butter sandwiches and chocolate malts before he made the five-hour trip to his dorm in August. Wendell planned to drive Steve to college, and I wasn't invited this time, either.

"Sorry I'm late," Steve said. "I had to take Luke to band practice."

Steve looked great, sporting a dark, trimmed beard. *My baby has a goatee!* His deep blue eyes crinkled with kindness, while the musical tenor of his voice washed over me. We visited a short time, and then he had to go. I handed Steve a small paper sack containing his college bank statement, a Walmart gift card to fix up his dorm room, and a typed love letter. He chauffeured me the few blocks back to where I had parked.

I watched one of the loves of my life drive off into his future, with his broad shoulders filling the cab of the Chevy, wind blowing through his black hair, and his hand confidently resting on the steering wheel. Waving, with a fake smile on my face, I waited to cry until after he turned the corner.

How long would I have to wait to see him again? This agony of good-bye echoed my yearning for Luke. Although I tried to be strong, another slump threatened to overwhelm me.

The next day, I sat at the breakfast table and greeted another weekend alone. I toyed with the idea of phoning Tom, regretting that his number rested somewhere in a landfill. Craziness made me want to scream to any man on the street, "I need someone! Will you love me? If love isn't an option, I'd settle for company."

I shook my head at the insanity. No human could heal me. I had to face my grief and practice the principles of recovery, without the complications of romance.

Dear Lord, I need a friend right now.

Almost immediately, God answered in my heart: *I'll be your friend.*

"I know you are my friend, but I really need someone who can hug me, someone I can talk out loud to without worrying about needing psychiatric help."

I sensed his sadness at being rejected, but I was too busy with my own hurt to consider his. How could the Creator of the universe understand loneliness?

But I guess he did, because a moment later the phone rang with a call from my friend and neighbor, Robin.

"Hey," she said. "What are you doing?"

"I'm sitting here, sulking in my pajamas."

"Want some company? My boys are with their dad this weekend, and I'm lonely."

"Me too."

Robin drove over and came inside. She slumped in the chair across the table from me. Her faded pink bedroom slippers and old cotton pajamas fit comfortably with my gloom. We looked pitiful, but the situation wasn't hopeless. We stared at each other a moment, then we had to laugh.

God in his mercy had brought the two of us together to comfort each other. Looking at Robin's kind brown eyes, I said, "Let's go do something. Sitting around moping isn't helping either of us."

"I do need to get some things from the store."

"Me too. I have to pick up a hose and sprinkler for the yard."

"I've got an extra sprinkler. I'll run home, get dressed, and bring the sprinkler back. Then we can go to the store for other stuff."

Energized by her plan, I rallied to shower and put on street clothes. We shopped, then ate lunch at a restaurant. Activity had worked to defeat our depression. Robin reminded me to be grateful for the gift of a girlfriend.

Back home after shopping, I attached the hose to the sprinkler and turned on the water. The sprinkler spluttered and stopped. Now what? This little glitch frustrated me. All I wanted was to water the yard. Was that so hard?

Nudging the piece of metal with my toe, I leaned down to pick it up. Wendell or the boys would have had the equipment working in minutes, but I had no clue what to do. Time for humility—again.

I hollered at my next-door neighbor working in his yard, "Hey, Leon, could you please help me fix this sprinkler?"

Leon fiddled with the gadget while his wife Libby and I visited. He fussed over the equipment for thirty minutes, using pliers to loosen the spring. I grew embarrassed to impose on his time since he worked two jobs and needed to finish mowing his own yard.

"Hey, Leon, it's OK. I can run to the store and get another one."

"I'll keep working until I feel like cussing, then it's time to quit."

Libby chimed in with her Southern drawl, "Even then, he won't quit."

Perseverance is an admirable trait, one you also need to make the emotional and spiritual adjustments required to move from the status of wife or husband to being divorced. The death of your marriage causes deep mourning, usually without the benefit of a widow or widower's social support. You are dealing with a complete loss of identity, and only with God's comfort will you find the ability to heal.

Leon hunched over the sprinkler in determination, while Libby and I watched their toddler waddle around in diapers.

"Aha!" Leon said, squirting Libby "accidentally" with a little water from the hose in his hand. She smiled. Their love was a gentle, secure one. Would I ever have that?

Leon leaned over to attach the sprinkler to the hose. His glasses fogged with water droplets as spray misted him from the repaired gadget. Smiling with satisfaction, he watched the sprinkler spin round and round.

My thoughts chased each other in circles too. How long would I have to grieve alone?

Dear Lord, I need you so much. Please help me tough out the pain and go deeper to heal inner hurts driving destructive choices. I want to stop repeating cycles of dependence, control, neediness, and manipulation. I pray for courage to keep learning and growing. Thanks for sending people to help. I know you will never leave or forsake me. Amen.

At dusk, I moved the sprinkler to the backyard. Then I sat in my lawn chair and watched the sprinkler rotate. Click. Click. Click. Beside my chair rested a furry sentinel, with his paw on my right foot so I couldn't go anywhere without him knowing. Contentment filled my heart.

Healing takes lots of time, but when peacefulness fills you, you'll know you're making great progress. Recovery isn't an absence of problems. Instead, it is the ability to find satisfaction where you are. You have created a place of safety and can flourish in that setting. Although you'd enjoy the companionship of a significant other, you feel complete being alone.

As fireflies danced before the velvet night, I reflected on something Robin had shared earlier in the day. "It's because we are alone, and we have no choice but to focus on ourselves, that we can do the labor of healing. God's working on us. We'll get through this if we trust him to help."

God's presence felt particularly close that evening. Somehow, through the trials of separation and pending divorce, my religious beliefs transformed from seeing God as a remote, angry judge ready to punish, to knowing him as a vulnerable being who enjoyed spending time with me. The maker of the universe *liked* me, even though he knew my flaws.

God kept me company as I watched water refresh the earth and listened to crickets sing. He and I enjoyed a fireworks show of rising stars in an intimate quiet, not needing to say a word. Experiencing God as my friend filled the spiritual vacuum created in my rebellious youth.

Much of your healing will occur in the fellowship of other people—old friends, new acquaintances, neighbors, church, family, and support groups—but without the steadfast assurance of God's loving presence, you will not be whole.

Where are you in your relationship with God? Have you come to rely on his tender mercy or do you still try to earn his affection? Take a moment to imagine gentle, loving arms wrapping around you in a tender embrace. The Lord's affection for you is genuine, without limit or demand.

Healing Practice #9: Avoid escaping into new romantic relationships that may limit the process of healing and self-discovery.

Being alone requires a great deal of discipline and strength. Develop a romance with God to gain a deeper understanding of how special and loved you are.

Study Questions

1. Are you tempted to escape into a romantic relationship to ease the pain you feel? If so, what could be possible risks to your long-term well-being?

2. Without the distractions of another person, what attention can you devote to yourself? What new interests might you explore?

3. What relationship skills can you learn from friendships that don't involve romance? How do sexual interests cloud judgment about the overall emotional health of a relationship?

4. Analyze the relationship your parents have. How have you repeated their patterns? Accept the good ways of relating and think about how weaknesses can be removed.

5. Speaking up about concerns involves risk. How do you know when you should talk about a problem? See if you can create a math equation for addressing issues (e.g., Love + Tact = Honest Dialogue).

6. What lies have you believed about yourself that drove you to make destructive choices? For example, did you believe you were ugly, so you settled for anyone who paid attention to you? In facing deep pain, what are you learning is good about you?

7. How does belief in God's love affect the ability to learn, grow, and change? What is the biggest obstacle you face in your faith?

Resources

Day of Discovery offers a four-part DVD series about domestic violence in marriages. "When Love Hurts: Understanding and Healing Domestic Abuse" covers topics such as when abuse is worse than divorce, issues about submission, when apologies are dangerous, and when the church is needed most. Preview these at http://www.dod.org/products/DOD2049.aspx.

Steve and Celestia Tracy's ministry, Mending the Soul, provides Christian curriculum about healing from abuse. Their site is http://www.mendingthesoul.org/leadership-team/. For more information, call 866-535-5044.

Elizabeth Kubler-Ross wrote about five common stages of grief in her book *On Death and Dying* (Scribner, First Edition 1997). Denial is the first stage, followed by anger, then bargaining. Next, comes depression, with acceptance being the last phase. In many ways, dealing with the death of a relationship follows these same emotional patterns. Alan Chapman reinterpreted Kubler-Ross' stages in 2006, applying them to effects of any life trauma. For more information, see http://www.businessballs.com/elisabeth_kubler_ross_five_stages_of_grief.htm.

CHAPTER | TEN

CAPABLE OF
SELF-DEFENSE

*G*od's love surrounds you, but he won't put you in a glass bubble to insulate you from the world. He equips you with strength and enables you to take his message of love to others in need. He encourages you to face your weaknesses and shows you how to overcome forces of darkness.

I wanted to be happy and bubbly, but I battled bitterness about Wendell's unkind treatment. August completed eight months of separation, and the legal proceedings seemed endless. Because Wendell and I disagreed about property, our case had to go to the circuit court's full docket, which was booking hearings for the following summer—another year away!

In the interim, I wondered what I should call the person who had been a critical part of my life since youth. Maybe I should dub him "Mr. X," in the fashion Malcolm X used to reflect lost heritage due to slavery. Mr. X symbolized the destruction of dreams and hopes when Wendell made the Jekyll-Hyde transformation from charming to cruel.

One huge concern I had revolved around physical safety. At times, I feared Mr. X might come after me because I had the audacity to leave. Even though I lived with neighbors close by and the dogs would alert me to a trespasser, I didn't feel safe.

Rather than cower in fear, I registered for a women's program, cosponsored by the local library and police department, which offered instruction in basic self-defense. The class included role-playing for solutions in potentially dangerous situations, such as an attempted rape.

In one session, I learned my 120-pound frame, using simple twists, could throw off a 260-pound male attacker. The course objective wasn't to create martial arts ninjas; instead, the curriculum emphasized common sense and repetitive physical gestures to prepare women mentally and improve their chances of escape.

"Survival is the goal," the instructor said. "We want you to walk out of the situation alive. If that means you defend yourself, great. If it means you decide compliance is the only way you can live, we'll not hold that against you."

His coaching struck a deep chord, and through those comforting words, I finally found healing for the guilt and shame I'd felt since the post-honeymoon attack many years ago. Rape involved destructive domination, which hurt, particularly when the attacker was a spouse who should have been sharing an intimate act of love.

With the training drills came full recall of that initial violent episode with Wendell. For the first time in decades, vivid scenes blocked from memory came back. *How could I have forgotten the horror?*

No answer came, but the flashbacks gave significance to every training exercise. I disciplined myself to face the memories, applying the lessons diligently so I'd never need to experience that kind of helplessness again.

As I soon realized, practice allows you to grow more comfortable being assertive. Healthy people don't mind when you ask them questions. Instead, they respect your ability to analyze situations and enjoy seeing you succeed.

After one class, I asked the instructor if he would show me how to break a choke hold. He gave me a curious look, but I didn't elaborate. Then he moved in front of me, putting a hand on either side of my throat. I gulped at the closeness of his large body, catching a whiff of his deodorant.

He showed me weak spots in his hands and places where I could break his grip. The whole exercise took only seconds, yet this new knowledge erased a terror I'd had for decades.

In addition to physical skills, I also gained legal knowledge. The class handbook defined abduction as removing someone's personal freedom of movement. This included blocking someone's ability to leave a room. The unlawful restraint of a person by force, threat, and/or intimidation qualified as a felony. It surprised me that no physical harm had to occur for danger to be considered valid.

Another concern I had involved the fact that my phone would ring repeatedly around midnight each night. I let the answering machine screen calls, but as soon as the machine turned on, the caller disconnected. The phone rang as many as twenty-one times a night. Jarred awake, I lay in fear.

Did Steve or Luke need me? Was there an emergency? If so, surely my family would leave a message.

Was Mr. X scouting to see if I was home? Neighbors had told me a man in a gray van, which was what Wendell drove, had been parking and waiting in the woods by the entrance of the cul-de-sac.

The possibility of Wendell stalking me was disturbing, and the ringing phone went unanswered.

I'd learned in the Sunday school class to ignore that kind of harassment, whoever it came from. But I didn't want the problem to continue, so I contacted the police and asked what to do.

"You can get a protection order, if you can document the source of the harassment," the officer said.

So I added a caller-identification feature to my phone service and also took advantage of a free offer by the sheriff's office to have a home-security inspection. The service pinpointed vulnerable areas around residences, such as overgrown bushes or windows accessible to break-ins. The female deputy who conducted the check offered encouragement, giving pointers on simple safety measures.

"Is there a specific reason you're concerned about security?" the deputy asked.

"Yes. I've separated from my husband and I'm afraid he might come after me."

"You can get a no-trespassing order."

"What's that?"

"It's a letter signed by the magistrate, based upon reasonable cause, which prevents someone from coming on your property. Your husband has to be notified of the order. After that, if he so much as steps foot into your yard, a deputy can arrest him."

"Does the order cost much? My finances are pretty tight."

"No, it's free. Just visit the magistrate and explain what's going on."

"Thanks for the information."

After the deputy left, I got in the car and drove to the magistrate's office.

The female magistrate listened as I explained my situation. She looked doubtful until she heard that I'd bought my own residence, taken self-defense classes, and learned about the legal procedure from a deputy who'd inspected my home for safety. At the last comment, the official reached for a form, filled it out and handed it to me. "Make sure your husband gets a copy of this. It prevents him from going on your property at any time."

The whole process took only about fifteen minutes, and I felt better with the extra protection, even if it was only a piece of paper. Implementing security measures empowered me. Just as the self-defense classes taught, I had placed my feet in a firm stance and stood ready for whatever life might try to hit me with next.

Like me, you also probably would rather be Sleeping Beauty awakened by a gentle kiss or Cinderella being whisked away by the handsome prince. But many dragons exist in the world, and it doesn't hurt to have a few tricks up your ruffled sleeve.

Using Humor as a Tool

Having a sense of humor also benefits you in recovery. Back in the old days when you felt like a victim, finding the funny side of life seemed hard because you were too busy running from trouble. As you feel more secure, you can afford to laugh at the crazy situations you find yourself in as your spouse flails around trying to corral you back into submission.

Despite the complex legal battles swirling around me for custody of Luke—Steve already had turned eighteen—and disposition of marital assets, the assurance of God's love allowed me to wait calmly to see how he would resolve the issues at hand. Rather than give in to worry, I entertained myself by composing a modern fairy tale to capture the present scenario.

Once upon a time, there was a little pig and a big, bad wolf. To protect herself, the little pig ran away. The wolf was upset at first. After all, he had lost control. However, the wolf soon consoled himself by chasing other unsuspecting little oinkers. Meanwhile, the first little pig moved to a different house with white vinyl siding.

Occasionally, the wolf sent e-mails to the little pig, but she deleted them unopened. Then the wolf mailed a certified letter, but the little pig figured nothing nice would be in the package so she marked "refused" on the envelope and put it back in the mailbox.

The little pig kept busy rebuilding her life. She found new friends and maintained contact with old ones. She didn't have time to think about the wolf, although sometimes she felt sad that their relationship had failed.

When reality hit the little pig that reconciliation with the wolf never would occur, she asked an attorney to finalize legal issues. She knew the wolf wouldn't be happy about sharing marital assets, but the little pig liked to go to market on occasion and wanted to be sure she could. The little pig left the wolf a phone message to that effect. Soon after, she came home to an answering machine blinking a flaming red recording.

"I told you if you left what's mine alone, I'd leave what was yours alone," the wolf huffed. "You wouldn't do that, so now I'm going after your house and car."

The little pig shivered at the wicked tone.

"I'm going to have your banker freeze all your assets, and I'm going to call the Internal Revenue Service and tell them you didn't report income," the wolf puffed. "And if you say again I have a problem with alcohol, I'm going to air your dirty laundry and tell everyone you have a prescription-drug addiction."

The little pig listened to the threats, wondering if the wolf's gusts would blow the house down. She waited a few minutes for her heart to stop racing, then she laughed. The big, bad wolf might blow and blow, but he was full of hot air. The little pig knew there was nothing to fear because she conducted her affairs with integrity.

She called her attorney and played the wolf's message so the harassment would be on record. The little pig then called her physician and asked for a letter documenting health records with no addiction problems. The little pig hoped the wolf wouldn't get asthma from hyperventilating.

Although the above fairy tale is a bit tongue in cheek, its message should remain clear.

Be vigilant about your safety at all times. Don't take for granted that an abuser will just give up and let you alone. An abuser has a huge ego at stake and might resort to dirty tricks to discredit or destroy you.

Clarity to Make Decisions

Without your typical cloud of sentimental affection, when you see nasty behavior from your spouse, you realize that your abuser really isn't capable of providing the love you need and deserve. You come to a crossroad where you wish your spouse well, but you cannot stand the thought of hanging around anymore for him or her to come to their senses. You have the clarity of mind to seek final closure to the relationship.

By autumn, I had taken action to end the limbo of almost a year of waiting. I told Hattie to file formal divorce proceedings, which would involve dividing the remaining financial assets. Though Wendell had bought out my portion of the original residence, he retained control of family business assets. If Wendell went after the car, which I'd bought with my teaching salary and held sole title to, he needed to share the value of his three vehicles, including his newly purchased convertible.

Ever since Wendell sent our joint income taxes late that one year, I'd been filing a separate return. I also had closed our joint credit card accounts and opened an individual checking account. Should a tax audit be required, my accountant could produce documents to show that all was in order, on my end at least.

Fortunately, I had taken those documents when I moved.

While Wendell's rage used to make me afraid, now he disgusted me. What made him think he owned everything? I wasn't on a vendetta. The courts would determine fair distribution. In the state we lived in, assets acquired by either person during a marriage belonged fifty-fifty to both.

Any decisions I made beyond Wendell's decrees angered him, and he responded with ferocity. The battle in court would be awful, but I refused to cave in to Wendell's intimidation. In this season of adversity, I'd discovered new abilities. Accustomed to financial hardship with Wendell's erratic spending, I knew how to manage money carefully and lived within the limits of my modest income.

Having the freedom to spend my own paycheck, without worrying about covering Wendell's unexpected expenses, pleased me. I also felt pride for not having to ask my parents for financial assistance, even though they would have been more than willing to help. Even so, they worried.

Dad called to check on me. "Are you doing OK financially?"

"I'm able to cover my bills. But if the court stuff continues, the attorney fees are going to be high."

"If you need anything, Mom and I are here for you."

"Thanks, Dad. That means a lot."

"Lydia, you are very resourceful," Dad said. "I've underestimated you."

His encouragement empowered me to keep marching forward.

From a reserved tolerance about me leaving Wendell to active support during Wendell's blatant jabs after our separation, my parents had watched my progress in the journey to independence. They honored my labor to take responsibility for myself.

Who are the people in your camp cheering you on? How do they let you know that they approve of your efforts toward self-determination? Consider phoning them today and thanking them for their support. Let them know much you appreciate them being valuable assets in your recovery.

Resilience Riding Out Storms

Maintaining a strong support network is a major factor in long-term recovery. You will need to tap every resource you have to buffer yourself against an abuser's fits of fury when he or she finally realizes that not only do you not want to be with them, but you are thriving without them.

They'll react to the rejection in unpredictable ways. Understand that they are so caught up in their own pain that they cannot reason how to work through issues and move on themselves. Often, all they can focus on is trying to punish you for failing to support them in the manner to which they grew accustomed. Some abusers go so far in their illness that they choose to try to destroy you, if they can't have you for themselves.

Physically and financially, I had taken strong measures to protect myself. With these paths blocked, Wendell attacked my reputation.

After work on a Tuesday in mid-September, I found a subpoena stuck in my front door. The document indicated Wendell had hired a second lawyer to allege that I'd embezzled money from Steve and Luke's college funds. Wendell's approach astounded me. He never contributed a single dime to these accounts, though he'd managed to buy a couple of airplanes and some ocean-going boats.

Even worse than Wendell's greed was that he had the attorney word the petition with Steve and Luke as the complainants. This attack caught me by surprise. What did the boys think?

I recalled talking with them last November about my using their college accounts for emergency cash to buy a separate house. Wendell knew about the transaction because I gave him the tax documents for filing. Why had he waited six months to start a civil lawsuit?

Since I found the document after Hattie's office had closed, I called Dad in a panic.

"I gave you that money a long time ago and told you to use it however you felt was appropriate," he said. "You did nothing wrong, and I'll stand in a court of law and say that to Wendell's face. How dare he try to use my generosity to hurt you!"

In the morning, I called my attorney, but her secretary said she was on the other line. Hattie never returned the call. That wasn't a good sign.

Three days later, at the pre-trial custody hearing with a new judge, Hattie presented my petition for joint custody due to several concerns. "Your honor, we'd like to request adult supervision for the boys after nine o'clock," she said.

"My client would testify under oath that the boys have never been left alone overnight," countered Wendell's lawyer.

A bald-faced lie!

"The boys have been left alone on several occasions," Hattie said, reading the dates on the list I'd given her.

The judge tipped his glasses toward his nose, looking down at Wendell. "That information will be presented at the full trial in a month."

How could the judge delay a decision without investigating concerns affecting Luke's well-being? What else might happen in the next four weeks?

The judge authorized psychological and substance-abuse screenings for Wendell and me. I didn't mind submitting to these, as I had nothing to hide.

When events careen out of control around you, stand your ground. Just as you have figured a way out of the muddle many times before, you will make it through this latest predicament.

Take a big breath, then let the air out slowly. Square your shoulders. Make a mental checklist of things that can be done, ask for assistance from trusted sources, and start exploring ways to solve the problem. You know you have the ability to meet the task, and you have God and your support network to help see you through.

Selfish Interests Set Aside

Being capable of self-defense is a good attribute, but you also need to be able to tell the difference between protecting yourself and justifying your behavior because of your selfish interests. Rigorous honesty with yourself is essential to full recovery. You have to be willing to look at your motives.

If you see shortcomings, address them and make appropriate amends. Test your heart before making decisions to ensure you are acting for the right reasons.

I had a clear conscience about how I'd managed money, but what I should do about custody for Luke remained a problem. How could I help parent and protect him when he refused contact with me?

A few weeks before the custody trial, Wendell brought Luke to a counseling session to talk with me. Hoping to break the stalemate with Luke and restore communication, I headed to the appointment. On the way, my Hyundai stopped at a red light. A sleek, silver convertible with the top down pulled up in the next lane. Inside sat Wendell and Luke. My heart sank. How could I compete with the lavish lifestyle Wendell offered?

When the light turned green, I continued on to the counseling office. Wendell and Luke parked a few spots away. None of us spoke as we walked to the entrance.

Once inside the small waiting room, we fidgeted. When the therapist finally waved us toward his meeting room, Wendell shouldered in ahead of me.

As soon as the counseling began, Luke made it clear that he did not want me as custodian, nor did he want to spend time with me. Wendell sat with folded arms, looking smug. At no point did Wendell encourage Luke to work things out with me.

Ed, the therapist, gently tried to remove barricades by encouraging Luke to address me directly. Luke parroted accusations, sounding just like Wendell.

After several heartbreaking moments, Luke's rigid posture collapsed into a childlike heap. With slumped shoulders, he said in an apologetic tone, "I just want to be with my dad. It's a guy thing."

The sadness in Luke's voice chilled me. I saw how the constant battle between Wendell and me was destroying our child. As much as I wanted to be with my son, I wasn't willing to tear him apart to get a little piece for myself. Like the woman fighting for a disputed child in King Solomon's day (1 Kings 3:16–28), I would rather step away than have Luke shattered by a power struggle between his parents.

"I don't want to disrespect the relationship between you and your dad, but I do want to ensure your safety. I'd like to have a relationship with you, and I'll wait patiently until you're ready. If you need anything, call me."

Ed looked at Luke. "The war between your parents is going to be dirty in court. You need to protect yourself and stay out of it."

Next Ed addressed Wendell. "Now, you won't punish Luke if he gets all cuddly with his mom, will you? You won't give him grief or not let him borrow the car?"

Emotion overwhelmed me. With Steve at college, Luke would be forced into isolation if he didn't have someone to drive him around. He still had a year to go before he could get his driver's license.

"Wendell, you'd better protect him and love him." I burst into tears.

Wendell looked at Ed. "She's bipolar, you know."

"I don't need your diagnosis," Ed said.

I got up and walked out into the hallway, wanting to find a tissue and collect my wits. Wendell soon joined me, saying Ed wanted to talk with Luke alone. There was nothing more to do, so I left. At least Luke had a chance to speak privately with the counselor to get a balanced perspective from a neutral observer.

At home, I collapsed onto the bed and wept. Like a drowning person reaching for a life preserver, I fumbled for my Bible on the bedside table. I opened to Psalm 44:3: "It was not by their sword that they won the land, nor did their arm bring them victory; it was your right hand, your arm, and the light of your face, for you loved them."

Only God could take care of Luke now. I rolled out of bed and stumbled toward the dresser, where two gilt frames held pictures of Steve and Luke in their basketball uniforms. I picked up the photos and crawled back onto the bedspread, curling into a fetal position and cradling the boys' images near my tummy. That was the closest I could get to hugging them.

This moment of despair tested how much I trusted God. Would anger, or confident hope, win?

I chose to set aside my selfish desire to be with my children if it freed them from being enmeshed in an ongoing tug-of-war. I accepted that God, as their heavenly parent, could ensure their well-being, even if I had to step back.

Despite months of recovery, facing this reality shook me. Yet I counted all the times that God had demonstrated caring for me. He'd brought me through many storms, and he'd do the same for my sons. Like Noah, I kept building my life on God's direction, knowing that when trouble flooded around me, I'd be able to rise above the danger and find safety (Genesis 7–9).

You can count on God too. He keeps his promises. Follow his guidance, be faithful to his commands, and watch for signs of his mercy. Wait patiently to see how he'll deliver you.

Healing Practice #10: Shield yourself with strong, supportive people to buffer against vicious attacks by abusers.

In high-stake situations, people who batter use physical and emotional violence to maintain control. Keep yourself protected and do not try to negotiate alone.

Study Questions

1. Who has supported you in times of crisis? What words of comfort have they given you?

2. Many fairy tales depict women as helpless and needing a rescuer. How do you feel about that stereotype? What measures can you take to protect yourself?

3. Is your spouse continuing to harass you? There may come a time when you need to completely disengage. When your spouse has consistently failed to demonstrate any desire to heal the relationship, it is time for you to stay totally apart. No matter how tempting it might be to take a phone call or plan a meeting, protect yourself. Don't entertain any communication that will only get you upset again and undermine your progress. Any response you give to an abuser rewards his or her effort and encourages him or her to keep bothering you.

4. Does any guilt linger for things you've done in the past to survive? Let that go. God understands your circumstances. He will not fault you for choosing a path you believed necessary to stay alive.

5. Think about times that you've been resourceful and made do with little. Think of the old saying "Want is the mother of invention." How have you used imagination to fill a need?

6. Has there ever been a time when your belief in God was the only thing that kept you from falling apart? What happened to encourage you to keep moving forward?

Resources

The Rape Aggression Defense Systems website is http://www. rad-systems.com. This program exists in most of the United States. The national RAD coordinator's number is 757-868-4400. Instruction is provided for women of all ages and physical ability. If you've ever had a physical confrontation, or if you want to invest in specialized training, contact this group.

The U.S. Department of Justice funds an Office for Victims of Crime, which compiles an online directory of organizations that assist victims of domestic abuse. The mailing address is 810 Seventh Street NW, Eighth Floor, Washington, DC 20531, or you can access the website at http://ovc.ncjrs.gov/findvictimservices/search.asp.

Choosing an attorney can be a complicated process, particularly if you feel uneducated and inadequate. Here is a link to a website with good suggestions for learning how to choose a lawyer to represent you and how to negotiate fees: http://www. expertlaw.com/library/consumer/howtohire.html#Q8.

The *Oxford Book of Modern Fairy Tales*, edited by Alison Lurie (Oxford University Press 1993), includes Jeanne Desy's short story titled "The Princess Who Stood on Her Own Two Feet." The tale offers insight into tactics that abusers use to gradually establish complete control over their victim. The full text is available at http://www.tallwomen.org/contents/princess.htm.

CHAPTER | ELEVEN

CALM IN CHAOS

*S*ometimes even the shoreline gets rocky. When you are facing times of upheaval, look back to see how many times God already has saved you and trust he will do so again. Experience has taught you that you can rely on God to carry you past danger. "Now faith is being sure of what we hope for and certain of what we do not see" (Hebrews 11:1).

These words of assurance from the Bible provided me great comfort as more unknowns loomed with the final custody hearing. The court date neared, and I met with Hattie on a Friday morning to prepare.

"Did Wendell provide the list of movie titles being shown at his home?" I asked, following up on concerns I'd expressed after finding Luke's note on the dresser.

"I did get a copy of the cable bill so we could document any pornographic movies being watched in the home," she said. "But all the titles are blacked out."

"How can they block the very information we've asked for?" My frustration mounted.

Hattie bristled. "I've done everything you asked me to do, but all you do is question me. We don't have a relationship of trust here."

So far, all the money I'd paid her had only resulted in a few five-minute phone calls and a couple of brief court appearances. The hearing was in four days; this was no time to get emotional. I took a deep breath and got control of myself. "I'm sure we could talk about our differences of opinion and work to resolve them."

"I'm not," Hattie said firmly. "I'm concerned that if the hearing results aren't what you want, you might lodge a complaint about me with the bar."

I hadn't seen that coming.

She slid a legal-looking paper across the desk toward me. "This is a form releasing me from your case. I want you to sign it."

How could she take so much money from me and then dump me? She made no mention of any refund due from the retainer, and I stood no chance of getting another lawyer in time to prepare for the hearing.

I left without signing the form, and the weekend passed in agony.

At court on Tuesday, Hattie arrived fifteen minutes before the hearing started.

"How are you?" she asked.

"Scared."

"No need to be. I protect my clients."

Had she reconsidered? Was she going to help me after all?

"All stand," the bailiff called in a solemn voice as the judge entered the courtroom.

"Your Honor," Hattie said, "we request postponement of this case."

Postponement? Hattie knew how important timing was to me.

The judge glared at Hattie. "This case has been set for months. You can withdraw, but you'd be leaving your client to represent herself."

Hattie leaned toward me and whispered, "Ask for a continuance, saying the reports required of the other party weren't turned in on time. There's stuff about Wendell on the substance-abuse evaluation you need to look at." She pushed a cardboard box full of papers toward me and walked out of the courtroom.

With Hattie's abandonment, terror washed over me. I looked at the empty chair beside me and prayed silently. *Dear Lord, you said Jesus will be my advocate, and I really need him right now. Please give me strength to handle this situation and the right words to say.*

You can do all the right things for a long time and still get kicked in your teeth. Shock registers throughout your system when yet another person you count on lets you down. You cry out to God, "Haven't I got through enough already?"

But don't despair. He has a plan, and he won't abandon you.

Trusting God as Your Advocate

The Israelites didn't understand why they had to wander in the desert, and Abraham had no clue why he had to offer up his precious son as a sacrifice (Exodus 15-16; Genesis 22). But God used those difficulties to develop obedience and strength in people he would later invite to be leaders.

Hardship makes or breaks you. You can steel yourself to endure what comes your way, all the while stretching your capacity for understanding and compassion, or you can wimp out and whine the rest of your life, wondering if you could have succeeded if only you'd kept going a bit longer.

You have what it takes to see recovery through to completion. Don't let the trials beat you down. Set your face like stone and keep your eyes on the finish line.

That is exactly what I did in the courtroom; I chose to make a stand. "Because the Sovereign Lord helps me, I will not be disgraced. Therefore have I set my face like flint, and I know I will not be put to shame" (Isaiah 50:7).

The only experience I had with legal proceedings came from watching Perry Mason on television as a kid. I glanced over my shoulder at the character witnesses who'd taken time off from work to testify on my behalf.

My therapist, Reba, sat beside my codependents-group mentor, Dolores. The pastor who led the divorce-recovery group stood beside my principal of four years. A long-term neighbor joined them to testify about my good care of the boys during the years Wendell lived out of state. I couldn't ask these people to make another trip, much less leave Luke to fend for himself.

"Your Honor," I said, "this case has been delayed too many times already. Would it be OK to proceed?"

The judge nodded, then he gave me brief instructions on what to do. So began four hours of wrangling with Wendell's lawyer. Every witness I called and every statement I made elicited an objection. But the judge repeatedly overruled, giving me opportunities to speak. My confidence grew. On several occasions when I questioned the other attorney's comments, the judge ruled in my favor.

However, in the chaotic pressure of the proceedings, I had no time to find the substance-abuse or psychological reports. Even if I had been able to find them in the stack of documents Hattie left, I didn't know how to interpret the scores. I wasn't sure whether the judge had seen them and forgot to ask him if he had.

After my character witnesses had spoken, the judge asked the guardian ad litem, an attorney assigned solely to represent the best interests of a minor, what Luke wanted.

"Your Honor, this young man is bright and articulate," the guardian said. "He's fifteen years old, plays varsity sports, and stays on the honor roll. And he wants to live with his dad."

"It's not often that this court has to decide between two such well-qualified parents," the judge said. Without proof of neglect, the court honored Luke's choice, and the judge ruled Wendell would have sole physical and legal custody. I didn't even get visitation rights.

"Because I am substituting on this bench, I am making this an interim order," the judge said. "The father has sole responsibility for coordinating communication and reconciliation between the son and mother. This effort will be evaluated when the case goes back on the docket for a final decision in a few months."

Why had I been so cocky to believe I could navigate the complexities of the judicial system? In shock, I stumbled toward Dolores, who had driven me to the courthouse and patiently waited throughout the long afternoon. Her head bowed in sympathy, she put her arm around me.

As we exited through the large wooden courtroom doors, the guardian ad litem told me, "You did a good job in there," and continued on her way. But her kindness did little to console me. All I could think about was that I'd lost any ability to protect Luke. I couldn't understand why God had allowed that to happen. What did the Lord know that I couldn't see?

Believing in God didn't mean I had a free ticket from trouble; instead, faith gave me the ability to handle trials differently. My former response of freezing in panic evolved into a calm outlook, waiting to see how God would move.

That night at home, I tried to see the situation from another angle. Positive points existed. Luke had an opportunity to express his wishes to the guardian ad litem representing him. My son knew I wanted to be with him and protect him. Wendell had formal accountability to the legal system for working to restore communication. None of these were exactly what I wanted, but I had to satisfy myself they were enough for the time being.

You might face a test like this that shakes you. You want to believe that God loves you and will reward your efforts to be good, but the immediate evidence looks bleak. Try to see past the disappointment.

Remember God said, "For I know the plans I have for you, plans to prosper you and not to harm you, plans to give you hope and a future" (Jeremiah 29:11).

Enduring Emotional and Psychological Abuse

Although you cling to hope, on some days you wish you hadn't gotten out of bed. You don't understand how your spouse can continue to devote such incredible energy to hurting you. All you want is peace. You've tried and tried to negotiate a cease fire, only to realize that more ammunition is being hurled at you.

That is exactly the situation I found myself in. Within a few days of being designated interim sole custodian of our younger son, Wendell demanded that I surrender to him Luke's birth certificate, Social Security card, and all financial assets held in Luke's name.

Wendell also scheduled an appointment with the principal of Luke's high school, who happened to be my boss. Claiming I had embarrassed Luke in the hallway by saying hi to him, Wendell asked the principal to prevent me from having any contact with Luke on school grounds.

I read the formal letter my principal wrote—with copies placed in my personnel file, as well as Luke's permanent student record—to Reba during a therapy session:

> According to his father, Luke has feelings of anger toward you. These feelings allegedly stem from his desire for an apology from you for what Luke feels was a betrayal for talking with a coach about his personal situation. The father has requested, for Luke's peace of mind, that you not interact with him here at school. The guidance counselor agreed this would be best for Luke, and I believe this to be a reasonable request, coming from the court-appointed custodial parent.

"That's ridiculous," I told Reba, looking up from the paper.

"What was that part about an incident with Luke's coach?"

"I talked with him in March the day after Luke didn't come home on time. I wanted him to know the stress Luke was facing with the family breaking up. How can Wendell take something several months old and blow it out of proportion?"

"That letter clearly shows that Wendell is trying to control all access to Luke. It also proves that you were in an abusive relationship with him."

Her statement shocked me. No one had ever said that to me before. How had I spent more than twenty years in an abusive marriage and never recognized the fact? Wendell and I had problems, but didn't everyone? Why did I always make excuses for my husband's inappropriate behavior? Worse, why had I doubted myself?

"Do you really think so? I mean, the only side you've heard is mine, though you did see him at court."

"The characteristics of people trapped in abusive relationships are low self-esteem, fearfulness, weakness, and lack of courage."

Those words definitely described the woman I was when I was married—and were the very same characteristics I'd been trying so hard to change since separating from Wendell.

"From what he's willing to do in broad view of everyone, there's no telling what he's capable of in private."

So all the pain I'd been hiding in my heart hadn't been such a secret after all. If Reba detected something wrong, who else had seen the signs?

"The fact that you were able to get out of that situation is remarkable."

Reba's words affirmed that I wasn't crazy and that my flight from Wendell had legitimate causes. But questions still remained. Could I keep trudging ahead, despite the obstacles? Or would Wendell's attacks destroy me?

People in abusive relationships often overlook problems as long as physical attacks don't occur regularly. This is a mistake. While laws define malicious wounding as the intent to cause grievous bodily harm, there's no pain like the emotional blow of being denied contact with your children.

Saying Hello More Than Good-bye

When someone else like a counselor recognizes your plight, and affirms you truly are in danger, you find the ability to keep your head up. You realize that you're not crazy, stupid, or bipolar. You understand that you are fighting for your very life.

A survival tool in this tense environment is valuing each and every moment as precious. Despite the hurts and losses, blessings still exist. In the middle of loss, you can focus on God and what he's doing—even if you don't understand—or sink back into bitterness, wailing about the past.

I'd worked too hard swimming above murky waters to allow myself to sink into depression again, so I used my coping skills to concentrate on the good things surrounding me.

Grateful for a holiday invitation, I celebrated Thanksgiving with several people from the codependents' group. Nine of us crowded around the table for a midday meal. Hospitality and joy filled the room. Even if we couldn't be with all our loved ones, we didn't have to be alone.

I missed Luke and Steve, but the generosity of my friends taught me that being a family was more than bloodlines. My new friends created such an inviting atmosphere that I forgot, at least for a little while, the sorrow of not seeing my sons.

That afternoon, I spent time with other members of my new "family." In addition to the codependents' group, I'd made new acquaintances at a clown school I'd started attending. A local church offered the free classes as part of a community outreach where volunteers visited the hospital to cheer up staff and patients. I decided to join because I needed laughter to offset all the tears.

Fighting off loneliness, I drove to the hospital, where I was to join one of my clown buddies in the lobby. I sauntered through the entrance wearing a polka-dot beret with my costume, and met up with Doc, who sported a green wig and lab coat. Together, we started rounds in the hospital.

"How do ya repair a tomato?" Doc quizzed patients along the hallway. After looks of puzzlement, he answered, "With tomato paste, of course!" He slapped his knee and stomped his oversized clown shoes.

People forgot their discomfort for a moment and smiled at my partner's antics. Feeling shy and slightly ridiculous in my getup, I hung in the background.

Two little boys poked their heads into the hallway. "Hey, what are you clowns doing here?" one hollered.

I peeked into their hospital room, where their parents nodded permission for me to enter. Between them, I saw a child who had to be the boys' little brother, swallowed up in the big hospital bed. The patient gave me a wan smile.

"Would you all like to learn a game?" I asked, waving a handful of peacock feathers.

The two older boys scooted closer and I showed them how I balanced a feather upright on my palm.

"Let me try," one boy said.

I bounced the upright feather off my hand toward him, but he missed catching it.

"You have to train your eye to watch the top," I said. "As soon as you have the feather steady, you can toss it to your brother."

Pushing out his bottom lip in concentration, the youngster tried again, this time catching the plume. While he practiced balancing, I took out another quill and moved toward the little guy on the bed.

His sad, pale face transformed when I tickled his hand with the soft tip. The parents grinned, and I handed the feather to him. Feeling good, I left to find my clown buddy.

Being around this brave family who supported each other in the middle of illness reminded me of many gifts God had showered on me. None of my relatives faced hospitalization. I had a job and safe place to live. Many people in the community embraced me, offering warm companionship. I had much to thank God for, even if all wasn't exactly as I had hoped.

When you examine your life today, what do you see that you can be grateful for? What changes have occurred over time, no matter how small, that indicate you're making progress? In the middle of facing good-byes, where can you offer a cheery hello?

Holding People Accountable

While you discipline yourself to see the good in life, you also need to hold others accountable for how their perspective impacts you. Establishing new expectations in relationships involves communication and sharing needs.

Often, you dodge a tricky conversation because you don't want to inconvenience someone. But the only way people will know how to treat you is if you teach them what you want.

For example, Steve had promised to tell me all about college when he was home for Thanksgiving. I thought he'd visit that night after I returned from visiting patients at the hospital, but he didn't come by or call.

Two days later, when he finally made it over, I intended to set him straight.

"Steve, I understand that it is costly for you to reach out to me. But if you can't be with me after we've made plans, please at least call."

"I'm sorry. It's just weird to come to your house. I have no identity here. But I guess that's because I don't spend much time with you. That's my fault."

I respected the way he responded with accountability. I grabbed his hand, led him into the living room, and showed him a beautiful Goebel porcelain statue of a woman cuddling a newborn in her arms.

"Your dad got this for me in Europe when he was stationed there before you were born. Now, there are some amazing things about that, the first of which is that a burly soldier would pick out such a dainty item."

Steve smiled and touched the figurine with his fingertip.

"Second, Wendell protected that fragile artwork the rest of his six-month deployment, bringing it safely across the ocean on a ship. When he gave it to me, we were planning for you to join our family. Those memories are some of the happiest times of my life."

The tortured look in Steve's eyes softened.

"I'm sorry I couldn't make the marriage work. I know that's hurt you terribly. But the past is done, and where we go from here is our choice."

Steve hugged me, and I reveled in his closeness.

Like holding feathers on your palm, love is a balancing game. You have to keep your eyes open and your heart ready to receive the pass.

Catch the tender look of adoration on your heavenly Father's face as he gazes toward you, admiring the way you extend his grace to others.

Healing Practice #11: Finding joy is a choice, no matter how difficult the circumstances surrounding you.

Where you place your focus often determines the direction your life takes. If you choose to see blessings from God, those good things will occupy your mind and help you combat discouragement.

Study Questions

1. Has anyone ever told you that you were involved in an abusive relationship? How did you respond?

2. When do you have a right to ask someone a difficult question? How can you discern another person's character based on the way he or she responds?

3. How might self-pity and bitterness be preventing you from finding happiness?

4. Have you ever given your best effort, only to realize it wasn't enough? How did you cope with the disappointment?

5. Have you experienced a court system? What was that like? What advice would you offer someone needing an attorney?

6. Look up Jeremiah 1:17–19 in the Bible. Think about this passage: "Today I have made you a fortified city, an iron pillar and a bronze wall to stand." In what ways have you felt God strengthen you?

7. Train your eye to see things for which you can be grateful. Try to come up with a list of at least twenty-five blessings. Write them down to remind yourself on dark days that things could be worse.

8. What are good strategies for holding someone accountable for his or her behavior in a loving way?

Resources

The Legal Services Corporation helps provide civil legal aid for low-income Americans in the nation. Nearly three out of four clients are women—many of whom are struggling to keep their children safe and their families together. For more information, call (202) 295-1500 or go to http://www.lsc.gov/about/about-legal-aid.

DivorceCare is a curriculum offered by many churches that helps people cope with the pain of separation and divorce. The twelve-week study pursues a biblical approach to healing and covers topics ranging from managing finances to sexuality. For more information, visit http://www.divorcecare.org/.

CHAPTER | TWELVE

Experiencing God's

Deliverance

When you are walking on the certain shore of God's love, you are prepared for whatever life might throw at you. You don't look for problems, but you feel competent to resolve concerns that might arise. This is a good mindset to have, particularly because life can take unexpected turns quickly.

After work one day in late fall, I went into the kitchen to find a snack. I pushed the play button on the answering machine and heard an unfamiliar man's voice say, "I'm an investigator with the state attorney's office. I'm looking into charges that you embezzled from your sons' custodial accounts. Please call me back as soon as you can."

My heart hammered as I dialed the number given.

"I'm confused," I said after introducing myself. "The matter you mentioned is already in the circuit court as a civil case."

"Well, ma'am, that may be, but it appears criminal charges may apply. Your husband brought in documents today for me to review. He and I talked a long time. I've heard his side. Now I'd like to hear yours."

I explained the history of the down payment on my home, adding, "I repaid the college funds in March."

"Regardless, it sounds like you've broken the law. If you're indicted, I'll be at your doorstep. In the meantime, I need to check a few more things."

I gulped, caught off balance with this development.

"Wendell told me he wants to reconcile with you," the investigator added.

Why would I want to go back to a man who sought my imprisonment?

"He said you abandoned him."

"Wendell agreed to a mutual separation last November," I said in a firm, controlled tone.

"I need to talk with my boss. I'll call you back."

"I would like to know what direction you plan to take as soon as possible. That will help reduce how many Tums I need."

"Pardon?"

"You know, the antacid medicine?"

"Oh, you have a sense of humor. OK. I'll call in a few days and let you know."

My composure lasted until the receiver hit the stand, then fearful thoughts rushed in. Indictment? Embezzlement? What would prison be like? How could I stand living inside a tiny cell?

I phoned my new attorney, a genteel older man with a calm demeanor. His secretary listened to my plight. "The soonest appointment I can get you is in three days. In the meantime, don't talk to that investigator anymore."

Right away I prayed for wisdom to know what the Lord wanted out of this situation and the ability to accept whatever that was. I asked for a Scripture, and Psalm 121 came to mind.

I lift up my eyes to the hills—here does my help come from?
My help comes from the Lord, the Maker of heaven and
earth. He will not let your foot slip—he who watches over

you will not slumber; indeed, he who watches over Israel will neither slumber nor sleep. The Lord watches over you. (Verses 1–5)

Staying home with the knowledge of a possible indictment would depress me, so I drove to the hospital where I volunteered once a week in the floral shop. Buckets of colorful blooms greeted me, and the fragrances in the quiet workroom soothed me. Creating beautiful arrangements brought me joy, particularly when I thought about the patients who might be cheered by the gifts.

After a few hours, I left the flower shop and drove to the YMCA to play volleyball. I loved the game, but had given it up years earlier when my sons got active in sports themselves and needed chauffeuring. Without that parental responsibility, I'd recently joined a coed league of average-level players who wanted to have fun.

Even in a recreational setting, the changes in my personality came out. In one game, a big male opposing player spiked the ball from the net, and the white missile barreled toward my face. Without time for conscious thought, my left arm moved forward, blocking the ball. I stood there stunned for a moment, and the play stopped as teammates shook their heads at the close call.

I marveled at how a few weeks of defense training had conditioned me to protect myself, even in an unlikely place. My self-esteem grew.

At home after the game, I enjoyed a peaceful sleep because I trusted God to work out the circumstances of my life in his way and his time. I knew he'd be with me no matter what.

In the morning, I thought about how this latest attack revealed Wendell's cold, calculated effort to hurt me. I felt certain he wasn't under the influence of alcohol when he visited that investigator. This clarified the underlying issues of control and manipulation I faced with Wendell. My estranged husband seemed bent on my destruction, and alcoholism had nothing to do with his motive.

As a police detective with a decade of experience said, "In cases of homicide or robbery, the event happens, but then it's over. The unique thing about domestic violence is that the threat is ongoing—sometimes for years."[51]

Wendell had hit a new low with this latest allegation of criminal activity. I had to give him credit for his persistence, but I certainly couldn't explain away such abuse with the tired old excuse of his drinking.

The investigator called me at nine o'clock in the morning. "I got copies of Wendell's complaint and your response filed at the circuit court. It appears as though you did rectify the situation by paying back the funds."

I released the breath I'd been holding.

"Had you not repaid the money, there would be a window for concern. But since you did, this case would be better handled at the civil level, rather than the criminal."

What had God used to influence this outcome? Had my straightforward approach convinced the investigator I had nothing to hide?

Maybe my new attorney's response removed any notion of wrongdoing. What might have happened if I hadn't been able to afford hiring an attorney to represent me?

As public awareness about domestic violence grows, new partnerships form. To address complex legal situations surrounding abuse, officials in King George County, Virginia formed an interagency task force that includes representatives from law enforcement, the court system, social services, the library, a large local employer, and victim services organizations.

Even the sheriff and a judge participate in this model for coordinated community response that has been recognized by the state office of the attorney general. The task force offers training to community leaders, including area ministers.

"We're all concerned," said an official from King George County. "We see the progressive problem of domestic violence. We've got to work as a community to solve these issues."[52]

God also works on our behalf, but trusting him to redeem negative circumstances requires great faith. Sometimes, his timetable doesn't make sense to us.

During the waiting, our beliefs get refined. I realized that my love for God wasn't based on receiving blessings, but on an absolute conviction that he would turn any evil into good. I believed that I was loved for myself, despite my imperfections. This knowledge banished any lingering doubts about my worth as an individual.

From what impossible situation has God delivered you? How can you share that story with others to offer them encouragement?

Seeing Beyond Material Value

As a victim you lose so much, but as a survivor you gain a richer life. Celebrating what you have in this moment frees you to see more gifts from the Lord.

His storehouse contains vast provisions that go far beyond glittery trinkets. With the fullness of recovery, you see the riches at your fingertips that many others miss. You have wisdom, hope, strength, and compassion. These jewels rival the contents of any castle.

As you open the present of opportunity, gladly share it with the entire family of humanity. This process leads to the discovery of many more precious items.

With Christmas just nineteen days away, I focused on things that had lasting value. Resigned to losing touch with Luke until God restored him to me, I threw myself into nurturing my high school students. They returned the affection. One thoughtful student who bagged groceries at the store where I shopped brought me a toothbrush I'd bought but forgotten at checkout.

My students and I studied stories about gifts and genuine affection. For a craft activity, I gave the students squares of colored paper and asked them to draw a present for someone special. Then they wrote on the picture what valuable item they would give. No one suggested frankincense, but these modern-day magi offered the following:

If I could, I would give the gift of truth. Because the truth will set you free. (P.S.: I lost your textbook.)

I believe the most valuable gift would be a second chance to those who would give anything to change their mistakes.

I'd give the gift of a dream so you'd know exactly what you want out of life and not waste a moment of it.

If I could give someone a valuable gift, it would be my trust.

I would give the gift of my love. I would be true to my word and someone others can count on.

I'd give the gift of praying for someone who was mean so they'd feel what it's like to have someone love them.

A valuable gift I would give would be a Tic Tac breath mint.

Those fifteen-year-olds had captured the wisdom of the ages with their thoughtful responses. I posted their drawings around the classroom to remind us of what mattered. And I took a breath mint, just in case.

Delighting in Good, Not Evil

Though you are moving forward, admiring the wealth of experiences unfolding before you, sometimes you will be tempted to look back over your shoulder. You'll chide yourself for having fun. A little sneaky whisper might say, "How can you enjoy yourself when your marriage ruptured and you are estranged from loved ones?"

Don't let that old guilt infiltrate your hard-won victory. There's no reason to sabotage the success you've achieved. God doesn't want you to mope around looking like a wreck. That doesn't bring him any glory or reflect the bounty of his kingdom.

Analyze your progress and reassess your goals, but don't backslide into feeling responsible for things you cannot control, such as your spouse's willingness to grow.

In my case, I thought about whether I had done every-thing possible to restore my marriage. Was there anything else I needed to attempt, so that years from now, I wouldn't look back with regret?

In church on Sunday, I saw my retired pastor friend, Brian. "How are you doing?" he asked before the service started.

"It looks like divorce is the only solution, and I'm torn."

"Lydia, if you seek divorce, you are stepping outside of God's will. Who will pray for Wendell's soul if you don't?"

Can't I pray for Wendell without being subjected to abuse?

Brian added, "I know of a woman whose faith was so strong, she prayed for her husband even though he tormented her. That man would pour cold water over his wife's head while she prayed, but she kept praying."

Did being a Christian mean enduring abuse? How could tolerating inappropriate behavior lead someone to Christ? Or was I a second-rate believer who couldn't handle persecution?

"I do pray for Wendell. But I'm tired of being a wife who's not honored."

"Read First Corinthians thirteen in the Bible. Then pray."

Have you ever had a minister or other respected counselor give you advice like Brian gave me? Doesn't that cause a horrible feeling in your gut? You want to be faithful, but you know that going back to the old routine would put you in jeopardy.

Although others mean well, sometimes they don't fully grasp your situation. Their limited scope of experience prevents them from understanding what you've already endured.

Due to the high number of police calls involving domestic violence, the City of Phoenix commissioned a research group to study women in shelters. Councilwoman Peggy Bilsten said in a Day of Discovery interview that most women in the shelters had a spiritual background, but of those who had approached their religious organization, only 7 percent actually received help.[53]

Weigh carefully suggestions offered by others, but know that God has given you a good mind capable of making the right decision for you. In the case of conflicting recommendations, you have to go directly to God. Petition him for answers and listen carefully. I went to my chair, sat down, and looked up the passage Brian had mentioned.

Love is patient, love is kind. It does not envy, it does not boast, it is not proud. It is not rude, it is not self–seeking, it is not easily angered, it keeps no record of wrongs. Love does not delight in evil but rejoices with the truth. It always protects, always trusts, always hopes, always perseveres. (1 Corinthians 13:4–7)

Did these verses mean I should ignore wrongs? I'd tried that. But the repetition of bad behavior needed to stop.

Surely my speaking in honesty wasn't rude.

As for self-seeking, I wasn't looking for someone new. I just wanted to be treated with respect, something Wendell seemed unable to do.

When did a lack of assertiveness become wimping out?

Although I valued Brian's opinion, hanging around for more craziness with Wendell made no sense. If God loved me, he wouldn't want me to be mistreated. And God already had given Wendell plenty of opportunities to change.

After church that day, I went home and called Mom. She was a woman of deep faith and Christian conviction. A powerful prayer, she also had a gentle, forgiving soul.

"Mom, I don't know what to do." I explained the situation, trying not to cry.

"I need to pray about this," she said. "I don't want to say anything without praying first."

We hung up. Then I collapsed on the bed as conflicting emotions overwhelmed me. At least I had Mom's help; I didn't have to carry the burden alone.

Mom called an hour later. "If there'd been one time in the last year when Wendell showed love, I would say that minister was right. But there hasn't been. There have only been behaviors intended to hurt and punish you. When someone treats you like a doormat, that's not love."

As she spoke, I felt a burden lift as despair and hopelessness vanished.

"It was really hard to watch the erosion of your marriage," Mom said. "Each year, you lost a little more of who you were."

Mom's insight surprised me. I reflected on the many compromises I'd made to keep peace with Wendell.

"At some point you've got to be able to hear God for yourself," Mom advised.

"I know. But this is too huge to go it alone. I appreciate you praying for me. I'm going to go for a walk and sort things out."

My prayer for you is that your marriage can heal. Having said that, I also understand that true love requires two equal partners who commit to the hard work of honoring each other and rebuilding trust. You can do a lot of things, but you can't single-handedly repair a marriage.

Discerning God's Will

The full process of healing requires lots of reflection. Spend time thinking about what you have done, what you can do, and what you should do.

No one can give you the right answers. Others might make suggestions or offer advice, but ultimately you have to determine which solution is best for you because you are the one who's going to live with it the rest of your life. Don't feel rushed or pushed to any one conclusion.

Independence means having the freedom to ask yourself what you want, without the shadow of anyone else's expectations. The only limitations you need to accept are the ones you impose on yourself. You aren't a frightened hostage anymore.

You have proven yourself to be capable and fair. You also have the strength of character to assume responsibility for your choices, however they turn out.

These are the very things I had begun to realize about myself. After finishing my conversation with Mom, I hung up the phone and put leashes on the dogs. It felt good to get outside.

My retrievers zigzagged, pursuing intriguing scents, while I watched clouds coasting along, wishing I could float as effortlessly to my destination. What should I do?

Two strange barking dogs interrupted my thoughts as they ran under their fence into the road, chasing me and my pets.

Although these animals were smaller than mine, they made up for their size with their peskiness.

At first, the aggressors followed from a distance and just barked. When I urged my pets to keep moving, the other dogs grew bolder and closed in. The more I tried to appease them, the more aggressive the other animals became. They mistook my desire for peace as weakness—much like Wendell had done.

One of the strange dogs nipped at my smaller retriever's heels, and the bite made my dog whimper. That's when I got mad. Putting up with bad behavior did nothing to stop it, so I leaned down and grabbed a fistful of rocks by the road's edge. Turning toward the attackers, I raised my arm and threw the stones hard, making the animals howl and back off.

I wasn't pleased to hurt them, but a demonstration of strength appeared to be the only behavior aggressors understood. Negotiating with Wendell was like that; he took my patience as a signal to wreak more havoc. I had waited and waited, hoping for reconciliation and change. But Wendell's effort to get me arrested was the last straw.

The time had come for me to sign final divorce papers. Despite Wendell's harmful behaviors, part of me winced at ending the marriage. Hadn't I vowed "until death do us part"? My religious convictions had always stopped me before, and loyalty had glued me to a harmful situation for far too long.

As I considered a living death of continued separation with no end in sight—or any sign of willingness to change on Wendell's part—I realized it was ridiculous to cling to nonexistent hope.

The passage from First Corinthians thirteen echoed in my mind: "Love does not delight in evil but rejoices with the truth." The truth was, I no longer wanted to live with an untrustworthy, cruel person who actively sought to harm me.

God's Word presented a promise, not just an obligation. God's love protected me and served as a model for real affection. I didn't have to settle for abuse and neglect, bound by a twisted sense of one-way responsibility. The power of that little word no returned.

As I'd learned when I was eight years old standing up to my great-grandfather, I did not have to put up with inappropriate behavior. God loved me and he had equipped me with strength to stand up for myself. He didn't want me to be treated like dirt.

No, there wasn't anything else I could, or should, attempt to save the marriage. And no, Wendell wasn't going to change and become faithful. He couldn't even be kind. Making a decision didn't seem difficult anymore.

Dear Lord, I want to do what honors you. I forgive Wendell and pray for him. Please give me wisdom to know how to proceed. I don't want to be weak. You enabled David of the Bible to fight a giant using a small stone. He battled not for selfish gain, but for your honor.

How can I do that as a woman? Your Word says love always protects, always trusts, always hopes, always perseveres. Help me promote righteous behavior.

I pray you will keep me from meanness that would harm anyone. Please help me be steadfast in prayer for others and give me the conviction to throw rocks at jeering giants—if necessary. Amen.

Take time to pray and ask God for insights that relate to your situation. His creativity in communicating is limitless. He's been known to use a talking donkey (Numbers 22), fireless burning bush (Exodus 3), soaking-wet sheep skin (Judges 6), and disembodied handwriting on a wall (Daniel 5). God will honor your heartfelt inquiry and lead you to the right answer.

Rejoicing with Truth

Jesus told believers, "If you hold to my teaching, you are really my disciples. Then you will know the truth and the truth will set you free" (John 8:31–32).

When the time is right, you won't need to agonize anymore about what to do. You will know that you've done everything possible and will give yourself permission to stop jumping through the hoops of the should-have-could-have drill. With crystal clarity, you'll see where you are, know how you got there, and delight in that position because it's an honorable place to be.

As I headed home with my dogs, I realized God knew how hard I'd tried to make the marriage work. After twenty-one years, my faith had grown to the point where I believed God's mercy exceeded his desire to discipline.

God didn't remain enthroned in a remote place passing judgment; instead, he set aside his power to join humanity in a humble manger filled with straw, surrounded by the smell of manure. Jesus's gift brought redemption, no matter how great my shortcomings.

"I desire mercy, not sacrifice" (Matthew 9:13).

God didn't receive glory from me destroying myself to keep an unhealthy relationship going. With mercy, Jesus shielded me from accepting abuse and control as poor substitutes for love. I could stop allowing Wendell to treat me poorly because I knew God found me lovable.

Like a marathon runner nearing the end of an exhausting race, I raised my hands in victory, knowing I had done everything possible to honor my marriage vow. God allowed me to cross a finish line without shame.

God will do the same for you.

When I arrived home with the dogs, I found a box that had been delivered by parcel service at my front door. My heart beat faster when I saw Wendell's writing on the label. I picked up the package, hearing a tinkling sound as the contents shifted. Had Wendell sent a Christmas gift?

After taking the package to the kitchen, I set it on the table and opened the flaps. Inside I saw shattered pieces of ceramic Christmas ornaments made by Luke and Steve when they were little. Wendell had put the fragile objects in a large container with no protective wrapping. During shipment, things had shifted and broken. This was typical of Wendell's blatant disregard for what I valued.

Sinking to the floor, I picked through the broken parts, hoping to find something intact. As I sifted through the shiny fragments, I sobbed about seeing the boys' precious hand-painted objects in ruins.

But God didn't leave me alone in my sadness. At the bottom of the rubble, one lone toy soldier lay on his side. The soldier's uniform featured unusual colors: greenish brown trousers, a yellow vest, and a pink cap. Wavy lines of paint revealed a youngster's unsteady touch.

Will you soldier on until others are ready to join you changing destructive patterns?

My hand trembled as I picked up the little soldier, feeling blessed that at least one symbol of family history survived. I too could keep marching forward, believing God was powerful enough to restore my dreams of having my sons with me and being honored by a man who loved me with tenderness and respect.

You also have dreams that will be realized. You will be amazed at the wonderful places God takes you. With his love, you will go from being a scared person who is constantly dodging threats to being a secure individual who has faith and dares to explore opportunities.

Your past refines you; it doesn't have to define you. Hold God's hand and feel his gentle clasp secure you in a world of many unknowns.

Healing Practice #12: God transforms loss into blessing and redeems grief.

The trials you endure teach you strength. Adversity helps define what's valuable and refines faith at a deeper layer.

Study Questions

1. "There is no fear in love. But perfect love drives out fear, because fear has to do with punishment. The one who fears is not made perfect in love" (1 John 18). Think about this passage. How can you tell the difference between an action motivated by fear and one driven by love?

2. My dad once said to me, "God must get a headache from listening to all the idle chatter of people who pray

for him to do things that he has equipped them to do for themselves. When God created everything, I wonder if he made aspirin for himself." What do you think about this?

3. When looking at broken ornaments, you can give up or soldier on. What path will you choose?

4. How has God answered your prayers for help and reconciliation? In a season of seemingly endless waiting, what signs of hope do you see?

5. In the Bible, the book of Hosea tells about a shattered marriage and how God used that to teach his people about how much he loved. God said, "I will betroth you to me forever; I will betroth you in righteousness and justice, in love and compassion" (Hosea 2:19). Even if your spouse is not willing to restore the marriage, God claims you as his own, forever in faithfulness. You will not be alone.

Resources

Violence Among Us: Ministry to Families in Crisis is a book about healing from abusive relationships based on Christian principles. The authors, Brenda Branson and Paula J. Silva, offer counseling based on fifteen years of helping women in dysfunctional or abusive relationships.

For more information about pastoral resources, contact FOCUS Ministries Inc. at contactus@focusministries1.org or at P. O. Box 2014, Elmhurst, IL 60126. The phone number is 630-595-7023. The website is http://www.focusministries1.org.

Changing for Good is a great manual explaining the mental process of becoming willing to change patterns of addiction. The book, copyrighted in 1994 by Collins, is by James Prochaska, John Norcross, and Carlo Diclemente. Years of their doctoral research across longitudinal studies document elements of successful long-term recovery.

Epilogue

You might be wondering how my story ends. I'd like to tell you that Wendell and I were able to reconcile, but that didn't happen. Our divorce took a second full year to complete through the courts. At the last appearance for property settlement, Wendell sat in the row behind me while we waited for our case to be heard. I wrote a note to him, saying I was sorry our marriage ended and that I hoped one day we could admire our grandchildren together. I ended with gentle humor, saying, "And I hope you don't let the grandbabies suck on your nose when we can't find a pacifier, like you did with our boys."

I passed the note to Wendell. He scanned it, then abruptly left the courtroom. When he returned, red rimmed his eyes.

A few moments later we were called forward. He left my note on the bench as though he had never seen it. He never uttered a word to me.

I spent another year adjusting to life as a divorcée. Throughout that time, Steve and I grew closer. During the Christmas break of his sophomore year in college, he told me, "Mom, I didn't see it when you left, but I do now."

I didn't ask him to explain exactly what the "it" was. From his gentle tone, I heard forgiveness. I think he realized that I left the marriage because I had to. Steve didn't harbor bad feelings toward me, and he kept on loving his dad too.

My older son encouraged me to be patient about my relationship with Luke, saying, "It took me a while to figure things out. Give Luke time, and he'll come back to you."

Although many dreams had been shattered, God did not leave me empty. I realized I could stand on my own and support myself financially. I'd developed strong, satisfying connections with many people. I practiced speaking up about my needs and desires in open, direct statements and trusted my instincts. Pursuing new hobbies and professional goals made me a more interesting person.

A feeling of fullness is the best way I can describe knowing that you've recovered from abuse. You don't have time to be bitter because you're too busy enjoying an abundance of activities and intimate friendships. You feel content with yourself and self-doubt no longer plagues you. Total confidence in your ability and God's unconditional love dispel that old emptiness of living in someone else's shadow.

Looking back at my youthful insecurities, I saw how I had given Wendell affection too easily. With maturity, I learned to see past flashy romantic gestures. I didn't need an intimate partner anymore, but I felt strong enough to take the risk of trying again should I meet someone trustworthy.

A co-worker introduced me to a friend of hers named Henry, who had a solid faith in God. He started our friendship by sending me a piece of cheesecake he'd made himself. After that thoughtful gesture, he began a steady courtship that showed he respected me as a person and valued me highly.

Henry had to work hard to earn my adoration and trust. But he didn't shy away from difficult conversations. He honored my opinions, even when we disagreed. I could speak up about my preferences and not passively accept whatever he wanted. Yet Henry didn't give in to my every wish; he too could enforce healthy limits.

Over time, Henry demonstrated his dependability through a constant gentleness. He got to know my friends and attended church with me. I told him about how others' alcoholism had affected my life. He agreed to my request of no alcohol—period.

I also confided in him about the sexual trauma of my past. I set a boundary of no sexual intimacy outside marriage, and Henry respected my wishes, without argument.

Some people may think I was weird, but I had learned how easy it was for my body to entrap my heart. Intercourse is not just physical passion and release; it is the intertwining of souls.

Just as I had reclaimed ownership of my mind, I now also controlled my body.

Henry listened to my needs and honored them. We built our friendship on a mutual desire to please God.

When Henry proposed marriage, I hesitated. How could I be sure it was right when I'd been deceived before? He waited patiently for me to become secure.

On the hot June day that Luke graduated from high school, Henry accompanied me for moral support.

Luke gave a speech as a class officer. "I think you should do one thing every day that makes sense. One thing that you can definitely be sure of. One thing that you will not regret tomorrow. One thing that your mother would definitely approve of."

His composed delivery made me proud, and his gracious reference filled me with hope.

Henry patiently sat beside me for hours in the sweltering heat of the football stadium as we watched graduates cross a stage on the field. He never once complained.

After the ceremony, Henry took me to the farmers' market, where we ate fresh fruit. On the way back to my house, we made a contest of spitting seeds at roadside signs.

At home, Henry held me tenderly as the tears I'd kept at bay all day finally erupted. Feeling safe in his embrace, I realized that Henry offered a love that gave me dignity and honor, without demands. With joy in my heart, I gave him my answer.

We pursued marital counseling through our church and also with a family counselor to address the baggage we both carried. We wanted to be responsible in looking at tough issues.

The week before Henry and I were to marry, Luke stopped by my house to talk—his first visit with me since that March disagreement three and a half years prior. "Mom, are you sure you know what you're doing?"

His concern touched me. We had a great time together and talked about many things. I assured him that I was completely confident about marrying Henry. When Luke left, my heart filled with hope to see signs of reconnection with this beloved son.

Henry's grown daughter welcomed me into the family and helped me shop for a wedding dress. Unfortunately, Luke did not show up for the wedding. Steve consoled me, saying, "Luke just needs time on his own at college to see the bigger picture." I hoped he was right that Luke and I could reconcile.

Over the next two years, God helped Henry and me build a strong marriage. We had our share of arguments, but the conflicts never tanked into personal attacks or accusations. We practiced the communication skills we'd learned in counseling, focusing on the issues at hand and then working together to find a resolution that satisfied us both.

The summer after Luke's sophomore year at college, he called me again out of the blue. After we chatted for a few moments, he told me, "I went on a cross-country car trip this summer with a friend of mine. One night as I was driving, I noticed headlights approaching in my lane. I realized there'd be a head-on collision if I didn't do something. At the last minute, I swerved and barely missed the other car. That other vehicle never stopped. This close call got me to thinking, and I want to make things right with you."

I thanked God that my son was OK and that he desired reconciliation with me. "I love you very much," I said, "and that will never change. Please forgive me for the way my leaving caused you so much pain."

He accepted my apology, and we began anew. This long-awaited miracle occurred almost six years after that November night when I dropped the wine glasses off the balcony.

So you see, miracles are possible. If you keep working toward becoming healthy and let God lead you through the maze of doubts and fears, you will see the impossible happen.

As a new Christmas season approached, I took the precious ceramic soldier from the storage box to place it on the tree. The doorbell rang, and Henry opened the front door. When I looked up, Steve and Luke's tall frames filled the hallway as they smiled and entered.

"Would you all like to help decorate?" I asked.

"Sure," they said.

I handed the surviving toy soldier with the pink hat to Luke, who looked for a good spot on the tree to place the ornament. That simple physical act represented a true miracle because my sons and I were together again.

While I sorted other decorations on the carpet, I snuck peeks at my sons, who were now young men. As the fresh scent of pine perfumed the room, my heart filled with awe at this marvelous example of God's restoration. Holiday piano music encircled us as Luke and Steve bent to retrieve other objects from the box. Humming with joy, I watched them work.

All those holidays lost to separation and agony disappeared in a moment. I counted my blessings: Knowledge of God's love. Rediscovery of myself. Henry and security. And now, intimate connection with the children I had had to give up for a time, entrusting them to God's care.

Luke unpacked an electric model train, fussed with the track, and remarked, "Boring toy executives. Why'd they only make an oval track?"

Inwardly, I laughed. Indeed, our family had created a new path that made room for figure eights, loops, and crossovers. We'd have more travels as we negotiated a healthy future together.

While Luke and Henry worked side by side setting up the train, I pulled more ornaments from cardboard boxes laced with paper lining. These weren't expensive glass balls, but they were priceless because they had pictures of the boys' smiling faces when they were children glued onto corkboard and edged in gold glitter. I'd made these ornaments my first Christmas during the separation. They symbolized my loved ones being present, if only in my heart.

"I thought all my baby pictures were gone," Luke said.

"I've saved them for you. I made scrapbooks too. Would you like to see them?"

He nodded and sat on the couch. I handed over the books, and Luke studied the mementoes, smiling at newspaper clippings of athletic events and honor-roll report cards.

While Luke flipped through the pages and Steve napped on the couch, I prayed their hearts would heal from the pain of their parents' divorce.

Walking Forward with Confidence

Wendell sold the old residence and moved to the Midwest to be near his family after Luke graduated from high school. I've only seen Wendell once in five years, when I drove Luke to meet his dad at the airport a year ago. Wendell took one look at me and walked away, which made me feel rejected and sad all over again. It also made me even more grateful for Henry's unconditional love.

Wendell isn't ready to forgive me for leaving, and I've learned to accept that. I hope someday that will change so we can take turns cuddling chubby grandbabies together the way we once did with our sons. I pray God will show us how to walk the path of 1 Corinthians 13, each of us learning to give—and receive—kind, unselfish love.

Dear Lord, thank you for restoring hope, love, marriage, and children to me. Amen.

Acknowledgments

Tracy S. Deitz would like to express gratitude to:

Lydia, for having the courage to make changes and trusting me to share her story.

God, for loving us unconditionally.

Husbands who honor and cherish their wives.

Children who find the ability to forgive and rise above the devastation of dysfunctional childhoods.

Parents who help children overcome unhealthy generational patterns.

Family counselors who validate feelings and help those injured find wings to soar.

Members of Codependents Anonymous, who share grief and assist those in dysfunctional relationships move forward in recovery.

Members of writers' clubs, for their support and painstaking help with revisions.

Members of the Church of the Good Shepherd in Vienna, Virginia, who sponsored the fall 2010 Christian writer's workshop and covered the event in prayer.

Editor Kathy Ide, for keeping the story moving.

Members of Alcoholics Anonymous who offer their experience, hope, and strength.

Pastors who provide spiritual covering with prayers, tackle tough subjects in church, and shepherd a flock in pain.

Trish and Alison, for their crisis management and prayers.

Vinita Hampton Wright, for affirming that each of us has a story of the soul to tell.

The Rappahannock Council on Domestic Violence, for giving voice to those who have been silenced, and law enforcement officers who provide safety.

Linda Riddle of the Domestic Abuse Intervention Programs in Duluth, Paula Silva of FOCUS Ministries in Elmhurst, and Tammy J. Smith of Paradise Valley Community Church in Phoenix, for reviewing materials.

Steve and Celestia Tracy, for their ministry mending souls.

Members of Amazon's Project Team Two at CreateSpace who did a wonderful job designing and producing the manuscript.

Medical and academic researchers who delve into dark areas to share others' pain and find a way to heal alcoholism and abuse.

All the other wonderful people in our families, churches, and communities who remind us opportunities for growth exist everywhere, and no one is alone.

Notes

1. 2010 National Census of Domestic Violence Services retrieved 28 April 2011 at http://nnedv.org/docs/Census/DVCounts2010/ DVCounts10_NatlSummary_BW.pdf.

2. "Domestic Violence Facts" July 2007 retrieved 9 May 2011 from the Public Policy Office of the National Coalition Against Domestic Violence at http:// www.ncadv.org/files/DomesticViolenceFactSheet%28National%29.pdf.

3. Ulester Douglas, Dick Bathrick, and Phyllis Alesia Perry, "Deconstructing Male Violence Against Women," *Violence Against Women*, Volume 14, Number 2, February 2008, Pages 247-261 as retrieved 8 May 2011 at http:// www.menstoppingviolence.org/cgi-bin/MySQLdb?VIEW=/viewfiles/ view_document.txt&docid=35.

4. Personal notes taken during interviews 8 June and 12 July 2011.

5. "Understanding Intimate Partner Violence: 2006 Fact Sheet," Centers for Disease Control and Prevention retrieved 13 May 2011 at http://www. cdc.gov/ncipc/dvp/ipv_factsheet.pdf.

6. NIAAA *Spectrum*, Volume 3, Issue 1, Page 2, February 2011 as retrieved 9 May 2011 from the U.S. Department of Health and Human Services at http://www.spectrum.niaaa.nih.gov/media/pdf/NIAAA%20Spectrum_ Feb11_508.pdf.

7. Ibid.

8. Estimates of AA groups and members retrieved 20 November 2011 at http://www.aa.org/subpage.cfm?page=74.

9. Annual survey sponsored by the Substance Abuse and Mental Health Services Administration retrieved 5 July 2011 at http://www.oas.samhsa. gov/nsduh/2k7nsduh/2k7results.cfm#Ch7.

10. Keith C. Klostermann, "Substance Abuse and Intimate Partner Violence: Treatment Considerations" Substance Abuse Treatment, Prevention, and Policy, 2006; 1: 24, published online 2006 August 22. doi: 10.1186/1747- 597X-1-24 retrieved 27 May 2011 from the US National Library of

Medicine's PubMed at http://www.ncbi.nlm.nih.gov/pmc/articles/ PMC1564385/?tool=pmcentrez.

11.   William Fals-Stewart and Cheryl Kennedy, "Addressing Intimate Partner Violence in Substance-Abuse Treatment," *Journal of Substance Abuse Treatment*, Volume 29, Issue 1, Pages 5-17 (July 2005) retrieved 8 May 2011 at http://www.journalofsubstanceabusetreatment.com/article/ PIIS0740547205000620/fulltext#section1.

12.   Jeanne McCauley et al, "The 'Battering Syndrome': Prevalence and Clinical Characteristics of Domestic Violence in Primary Care Internal Medical Practitioners" published in *Annals of Internal Medicine* 15 November 1995 in Volume 123, Number 10 retrieved 28 April 2011 at http://www.annals.org/content/123/10/737.full.pdf+html.

13.   Amy S. Gottlieb, "Intimate Partner Violence: A Clinical Review of Screening and Intervention," *Women's Health*, September 2008, v4, i5, page 529 (11) as retrieved 12 May 2011 http://galenet.galegroup.com.proxy.crrl. org/servlet/HWRC/hits?docNum=A225453150&year2=&year1=2008&aci =flag&aii=flag&index3=KE&index2=KE&index1=KE&tcit=0_1_0_0_0_0&ind ex=BA&locID=crrl&rlt=2&text3=&text2=abuse&origSearch=false&text1=d omestic+&op2=AND&op1=AND&t=RK&s=11&r=d&items=0&o=&seconda ry=false&n=10&day2=&l=d&day1=&month2=&sgPhrase=false&month1= &searchTerm=2NTA&c=56&bucket=per.

14.   Ibid.

15.   "Affordable Care Act Ensures Women Receive Preventive Services at No Additional Cost," news release dated 1 August 2011 by the U.S. Department of Health and Human Services retrieved at http://www.hhs. gov/news/press/2011pres/08/20110801b.html.

16.   Robert Preidt, "Domestic Abuse Often Escapes Notice of ER Staff: Study," 18 March 2011, MedlinePlus, U.S. National Library of Medicine, National Institutes of Health retrieved 14 May 2011 at http://www.nlm.nih.gov/ medlineplus/news/fullstory_110027.html.

17.   "The Public Health Problem of Intimate Partner Violence" reported in the DELTA Program: Preventing Intimate Partner Violence in the United States by the Centers for Disease Control and Prevention National Center for

Injury Prevention and Control retrieved 5 July 2011 at http://www.cdc.gov/violenceprevention/pdf/DELTA_AAG-a.pdf.

18. Tian Dayton, *Emotional Sobriety: From Relationship Trauma to Resilience and Balance* (Health Communications, 2007) 149.

19. Personal correspondence 19 July 2011 via e-mail from Linda Riddle, executive director of the Domestic Abuse Intervention Programs (DAIP) in Duluth, MN.

20. Hilary Price, Rhymes with Orange, 18 May 2011, *Free Lance-Star*, Fredericksburg, VA.

21. "History of the Battered Women's Movement: Focus on Virginia" disseminated by the Virginia Sexual and Domestic Violence Action Alliance as retrieved 8 July 2011 at *www.vadv.org/Resources/bwmhistory.doc*.

22. Linda M. Peterman, Charlotte G. Dixon. *The Journal of Rehabilitation*. "Assessment of Men Who Batter Women." October-December 2001, Volume 67, i4 (5) as retrieved 12 May 2011 from Health and Wellness Resource Center at http://galenet.galegroup.com.proxy.crrl.org/servlet/HWRC/hits?docNum=A81759717&year2=&year1=&aci=flag&aii=flag&index3=KE&index2=KE&index1=KE&tcit=0_1_0_0_0_0&index=BA&locID=crrl&rlt=2&text3=batter&text2=who&origSearch=true&text1=men&op2=AND&op1=AND&t=RK&s=11&r=d&items=0&o=&secondary=false&n=10&day2=&l=d&day1=&month2=&sgPhrase=false&month1=&searchTerm=2NTA&c=1&bucket=per.

23. Peterman, *The Journal of Rehabilitation, 2*.

24. Yuan, N.P., Koss, M.P., & Stone, M. (March 2006). *The Psychological Consequences of Sexual Trauma*. Harrisburg, PA: VAWnet, a project of the National Resource Center on Domestic Violence/Pennsylvania Coalition Against Domestic Violence retrieved 8 May 2011 at http://www.vawnet.org.

25. Joseph M. Carver, "Love and the Stockholm Syndrome: The Mystery of Loving an Abuser (Part 1)" retrieved 29 April 2011 at http://counsellingresource.com/quizzes/stockholm/.

26. DWI Lawyer Directory retrieved 23 May 2011 at http://www.dwi.com/blood-alcohol-content.

27. National Domestic Violence Hotline's article titled "Safety Planning" retrieved 30 April 2011at http://www.thehotline.org/wp-content/uploads/2008/10/Safety-Planning-2.pdf.

28. David B. Merrill, "Alcoholism and Alcohol Abuse," Medline Plus, a service of the U.S. National Library of Medicine retrieved 13 May 2011 at http://www.nlm.nih.gov/medlineplus/ency/article/000944.htm.

29. Legal Momentum, The Women's Legal Defense and Education Fund retrieved 13 May 2011 at https://www.quickbase.com/db/bdy472as8?a=dr&r=pu&rl=ucc.

30. Indigo Real Estate Service v. Rousey, Court of Appeals of Washington, Division 1, 31 August 2009 retrieved 14 May 2011 at FindLaw http://case-law.findlaw.com/wa-court-of-appeals/1408162.html.

31. Keith Klostermann and Michelle L. Kelley, "Alcoholism and Intimate Partner Violence: Effects on Children's Psychosocial Adjustment," *International Journal of Environmental Research and Public Health,* 2009 December; 6(12): 3156–3168.
    Published online 2009 December 10. doi: 10.3390/ijerph6123156 retrieved 7 July 2011 from the U.S. National Library of Medicine's PubMed athttp://www.ncbi.nlm.nih.gov/pmc/articles/PMC2800341/?tool=pubmed #b1-ijerph-06-03156.

32. News article posted on the National Domestic Violence Hotline website about a poll conducted by the Allstate Foundation National Poll on Domestic Violence in 2004 retrieved 1 May 2011 at http://www.thehotline.org/get-educated/abuse-in-america/.

33. The National Domestic Abuse Hotline article titled "What is Domestic Abuse?" retrieved 1 May 2011 at http://www.thehotline.org/get-educated/what-is-domestic-violence/.

34. Ibid.

35. "Treatment for Male Batterers" library index retrieved 9 May 2011 at http://www.libraryindex.com/pages/2064/Treatment-Male-Batterers-TREATMENT-TYPES-BATTERERS.html.

36. Jill Cory and Karen McAndless-Davis, *When Love Hurts: A Woman's Guide to Understanding Abuse in Relationships* (New Westminster, BC: Womankind Press, 2008, second edition), 98-99.

37. Ibid, 72.

38. "Animal Cruelty and Family Violence: Making the Connection" posted on Alternatives to Domestic Aggression by the Catholic Social Services of Washtenaw County retrieved 8 May 2011 at http://www.csswashtenaw. org/ada/links/animaldv.html.

39. Harriet Lerner, PhD, *The Dance of Anger: A Woman's Guide to Changing the Patterns of Intimate Relationships* (New York: HarperCollins Publishers, Inc., 1997), 3.

40. Melody Beattie, *Codependents' Guide to the Twelve Steps* (New York: Prentice Hall Press, 1990), 189.

41. A Window Between Worlds at www.awbw.org, 310-396-0317 x210, or info@awbw.org.

42. Albert R. Roberts, *Crisis Intervention Handbook: Assessment, Treatment, Research* (New York: Oxford University Press, 2005), 3rd edition, 468-471 as retrieved 10 May 2011 at http://books.google.com/books?id=xhl2bo 0Gv1MC&pg=PA384&lpg=PA384&dq=albert+roberts+and+handbook+ of+domestic+violence+and+art+therapy+for+children&source=bl&ots =6sn1gd45cL&sig=FnQq_zNn7amNLhY-NGCN5YwdUDE&hl=en&ei=O6_ JTYRyiuHRAazEpe8H&sa=X&oi=book_result&ct=result&resnum=1&ved=0C CQQ6AEwAA#v=onepage&q&f=false.

43. Peterman, *The Journal of Rehabilitation*, 2.

44. Ibid.

45. Statistics on Sexual Assault retrieved 17 May 2011 at http://www.turning-pointservices.org/Sexual%20Assault%20-%20Statistics.htm.

46. http://www.drjoecarver.com/clients/49355/File/IdentifyingLosers.html retrieved 11 May 2011.

47. Lenore Walker, *The Battered Woman* (New York: William Morrow, 1980).

48. Personal notes taken during a class given by Wayne Wilson in Fredericksburg, VA.

49. Personal correspondence 19 July 2011 via e-mail with Linda Riddle, executive director of the Domestic Abuse Intervention Programs (DAIP) in Duluth, MN.

50. Alexis Phillips and Judith C. Daniluk, "Beyond 'Survivor': How Childhood Sexual Abuse Informs the Identity of Adult Women at the End of the Therapeutic Process," *Journal of Counseling and Development*, Spring 2004, v82, i2 page 177(8) retrieved 12 May 2011 at http://galenet.gale-group.com.proxy.crrl.org/servlet/HWRC/hits?docNum=A117425291&year2=&year1=&index3=KE&index2.

51. Personal notes taken 14 June 2011 from a Stafford County deputy during a training session for volunteers in a council for domestic violence.

52. Personal notes taken 25 October 2011 at training offered by the King George Domestic Violence Task Force.

53. "When Love Hurts: Understanding and Healing Domestic Abuse, When the Church is Needed Most, Part IV" Day of Discovery DVD series produced by Discovery House. Viewed online 10 June 2011 via http://www.dod.org/products/DOD2052.aspx.